6 45

OUT ON
A
BROKEN LIMB

F. LaGARD SMITH

D0060581

HARVEST HOUSE PUBLISHERS
Eugene, Oregon 97402

Back cover photo: Ron Hall

OUT ON A BROKEN LIMB

Copyright © 1986 by Harvest House Publishers
Eugene, Oregon 97402

Library of Congress Catalog Card Number 85-80484
Trade edition ISBN 0-89081-503-8
Cloth edition ISBN 0-89081-561-5

Printed in the United States of America.

Dedicated to my sisters,
Maybeth, Beverly, Sandra, and Melita,
with whom I have been privileged to share
my one life on earth

With appreciation to
Richardson R. Lynn and Cynthia Novak

PREFACE

This book is the result of a brief conversation I once had with a young law student. When I saw her on our campus some time ago, she was very excited about her new belief in reincarnation. She almost insisted that I read actress Shirley MacLaine's book *Out on a Limb*. "If you've read Shirley MacLaine's book," she exclaimed, "then you pretty much know where I'm coming from. She's got it all in there!" Nothing could have surprised me more than learning that this bright, thoughtful, all-American young woman had become fascinated with reincarnation. My curiosity aroused, I went to the local bookstore to buy "Shirley's book."

I found *Out on a Limb* to be captivating and well-written, but I was surprised to find that Ms. MacLaine's memoir was really a philosophical statement in support of reincarnation, New Age consciousness, and me-generation selfishness. Even more, I was amazed at Ms. MacLaine's attempt to blend her eclectic belief system with the Bible. In doing research for a book I had written, I had just finished spending six years of my life reading and studying the Bible in the minutest detail. I *knew* that it did not teach reincarnation, as Ms. MacLaine and her spiritual mentors were indicating. I *knew* that words were being put into Jesus' mouth that he never came close to saying. I *knew* that historical facts had been grossly distorted in an effort to justify reincarnationist beliefs.

This book wasn't just another celebrity's life story which I could put on the shelf with a shrug of the shoulders. It was one thing for a superstar to write about her personal belief in reincarnation, but trying to make it fit with Christianity was too outrageous to let pass unnoticed! As explanations for what will happen to us when we die, reincarnation and biblical resurrection couldn't be more in conflict. Either we live many times on this earth, as Shirley MacLaine believes, or we live only once, as the Bible clearly teaches. The issue is not just idle speculation about life after death: The truth about what happens to us when we die goes to the very heart of our *present* existence. It was not long after reading *Out on a Limb* that Ms. MacLaine's voluminous reading became *my* voluminous reading, and her all-night writing sessions became *my* all-night writing sessions.

The need to respond to Ms. MacLaine's widely publicized philosophy has been intensified by the publication of her latest book, *Dancing in the Light*. In it Ms. MacLaine continues to advocate a belief system which is not only highly speculative, but blatantly contrary to the truth. And with each talk show appearance about her books, her New-Age-reincarnationist ideas find their way into millions of homes and hearts.

Those who have read *Out on a Limb* and *Dancing in the Light* owe it to themselves to look at the other side—the side which Ms. MacLaine did not present. Those who have not read her books but who are pursuing their own quest for life's meaning will be challenged by close scrutiny of the crucial issues which Ms. MacLaine has raised. This is not merely a philosophical debate; it is not just a matter of Shirley MacLaine having her truth and I having mine. There is a truth about life and afterlife which is absolute, uncompromising, and knowable. Truth cannot be ignored with impunity, for life's deepest meaning and one's own personal destiny are at stake.

—F. LaGard Smith

CONTENTS

OUT ON
A
BROKEN
LIMB

CHAPTER ONE

NEIGHBORS—
WORLDS APART

*"Surely, if all the world was made for man, then man was
made for more than the world."*

—PIERRE ALEXANDRE DUPLESSIS

I LOOKED UP FROM SHIRLEY MACLAINE'S BOOK and
out my window. The scruffy Southern California coastal
mountains, with their tousled covering of brushy chapparal,
dropped off abruptly to the Malibu lagoon and the beach,
where the waves of the Pacific crashed in a never-ending
sequence against the shore. From my vantage point high
above the beach in my living room, I could not hear the
sound of their crashing. Nor could I hear the cars on the
Pacific Coast Highway as they made their way along like
ants in a line. It was as if I were watching a silent movie.

Along that same Malibu beach, actress Shirley MacLaine
had struggled with the meaning of life. It was that beach
which formed the backdrop for Shirley's spiritual odyssey,
which she told so vividly in her memoir, *Out on a Limb*.
I too had walked that beach and shared those otherworld
times when the power of the ocean and the serenity of an
ending day made me question the meaning of life and the
universe.

And yet I was struck by the irony: Shirley MacLaine and

I may have walked the same beach, may have been almost neighbors, and may have had the same kind of philosophical questions, but from what I read in her book I knew that we were worlds apart in our conclusions about life. Shirley MacLaine believes in reincarnation, karma, communication with astral-plane entities through psychic mediums, UFO's, and extraterrestrials, all based solely on subjective experience, while I am more than ever convinced that Christianity is the key to life's meaning and the only true way to understand reality.

Our differences had ramifications broader than just our two private musings. As I looked across Santa Monica Bay toward Los Angeles, I thought of the thousands of people there and all around the world who had bought *Out on a Limb*, never suspecting that they were about to read an indoctrination manual in New Age philosophy. Even more unnerving was Ms. MacLaine's misuse and misunderstanding of the Bible, Christianity, and Jesus to support her ideas!

She is one of the outstanding actresses of our time, but I was astonished by her wild speculations about past and future lives. For example, there was the incredible passage about her own daughter:

> When the doctor brought her to me in the hospital bed on that afternoon in 1956, had she already lived many many times before, with other mothers? Had she, in fact, been one herself? Had she, in fact, ever been *my* mother? Was her one-hour-old face housing a soul perhaps millions of years old?

After reading and rereading her book over the last few months, and investigating the sources of her ideas and

Eastern thought, I find it hard to understand how a woman of Shirley MacLaine's intelligence and education could believe so many contradictory and frivolous ideas. Yet she is not alone. Thousands of people are turning to belief in reincarnation. We are in the midst of a "dawning" of a new age of "enlightenment" through Eastern practices of self-awareness and spiritual evolution. For centuries, while two-thirds of the world's population has believed in some form of reincarnation, it has not really touched Western civilization. Ancient Greek reincarnation ideas and those of such major religions as Hinduism and Buddhism have been fairly well insulated from Westerners. Now, dressed up in Judeo-Christian terminology and accented with the current fascination surrounding paranormal phenomena, reincarnation is sweeping through Western society.

For example, in a recent 12-page color supplement to *The Los Angeles Times*, the Hare Krishnas indicate that one out of four Americans today believes in past and future lives. "Reincarnation is fast becoming the most popular explanation of the afterlife," says the promotional. "A recent Gallup poll in America showed that now over 30% of people under 30 accept reincarnation as an explanation of life after death."

Poets, politicians, doctors, lawyers, and college students by the thousands who have left traditional churches are turning to Westernized versions of Eastern religious thought. Reincarnation is quickly becoming *the* religion of the so-called yuppies, many of whom attribute their interest in reincarnation to Ms. MacLaine's *Out on a Limb*.

The rapid spread of reincarnation as the fastest-growing religion in America sneaks up on people because it is a *belief*, not an organized system. There are no "First Reincarnation Church" buildings on the corner or "missionaries for the cause" knocking on our doors. Church buildings have been replaced by ashrams, storefront meeting rooms, gatherings in private homes, and classroom discussions. And the convert-seeking evangelists easily enter our homes and minds through a vast array of reincarnationist literature and widespread media exposure.

Our movie, television, and entertainment celebrities have popularized Eastern beliefs almost painlessly. Supersinger Tina Turner, for example, is a strong reincarnationist, and that belief is reflected in her recent release "I Might Have Been Queen" with such lines as "I'm a new pair of eyes, an original mind."

Shirley MacLaine herself is probably the most effective and popular crusader for the cause of reincarnation. Consider that *Out on a Limb* was on *The New York Times* bestseller list for over 15 weeks, and over two million copies have been sold. Ms. MacLaine promotes her philosophy before millions of viewers on such nationally televised programs as "Donahue" and "The Today Show." She says she has received over 40,000 letters from readers and viewers wanting to learn more about her reincarnation philosophy. *Out on a Limb* has been cited by other reincarnationists as "must reading" for anyone searching for life's answers. Without doubt, Shirley MacLaine is the Pied Piper of today's reincarnation tune.

Ms. MacLaine's latest book, *Dancing in the Light*, is an even more outrageous saga of her supposed past lives. She blithely assumes that previous incarnations have affected her relationships with her family and her various lovers. In *Dancing in the Light*, Ms. MacLaine goes even farther out on a limb. Under the influence of psychic acupuncture, she claims to be able to talk to animals, trees, and an entity which she calls "Higher Self." It is amazing to me that thousands of people would believe Shirley MacLaine when they wouldn't believe anybody else who happened to walk down the street claiming to be able to talk to trees!

Ms. MacLaine and I began our personal spiritual quests with radically different assumptions. I was raised by committed Christian parents, and my basic assumptions have always been strongly Christian. Regular church worship and Bible study were a significant part of my upbringing. My years of serious questioning about life—and testing the claims of the Bible—have only reinforced my belief in the Creator God of the Bible, the atoning death and resurrection of Jesus Christ, and the final resurrection of all the dead.

Although as a child Ms. MacLaine attended a Baptist church in Virginia and found the Bible to be fascinating reading, she was not brought up to be a religious person. Her parents sent her to church on Sundays because it seemed to them the place for her to be. In *Dancing in the Light* Ms. MacLaine says, "[My] so-called Baptist background (which was actually negligible) never really influenced me. After my first church picnic, I opted for necking on hayrides instead." From her father, a professor of psychology and education at Maryland College, Shirley may have learned as much about Plato as Christ. Perhaps that explains why Ms. MacLaine grew up thinking, as she says, that God and religion were mythological.

In looking for a spiritual substitute for organized religion, Ms. MacLaine has turned both to her own thoughts and to Eastern mysticism. What she has found in her quest for meaning and identity is a form of New Age consciousness and eclectic spiritualism. Her spiritualism fits particularly well with her belief that life's answers are not found in our addiction to technology, materialism, and political power structures.

Ms. MacLaine and I both agree that there is a spiritual dimension to life and to our existence. Man is more than a machine, and our world is more than a secular experience, no matter how much we ignore it or deny it. But there is great danger in her understanding of just what our spiritual world is all about—who God is, how we relate to him in this life, and what life is like after death.

What she advocates, and what thousands of people are accepting through her, is a belief system which will have profound adverse consequences to the very people who cling so tightly to it now, not only in this life but also in the life to follow after death. When talk-show hosts question Ms. MacLaine's reincarnation philosophy, she asks innocently, "What have you got to lose?" The answer is, nothing less than peace with God in this life and our own eternal spiritual destiny!

It would be one thing for Shirley MacLaine to decide what is true for *her* in her own life, although my concern for her as a fellow human being makes me want to share the truth I have found in Jesus Christ. But it is another thing altogether to play her speculative beliefs to such a wide audience, fully aware that thousands of people are entrusting their souls to the belief system which she has discovered. As she told Phil Donahue, others have been teaching reincarnation for centuries, but she is the one who is "making it more acceptable to the popular consciousness." Therefore she cannot so easily disclaim responsibility for what other people believe. And what she zealously promotes is so spiritually lethal that no one can afford to accept it without testing it.

Ms. MacLaine is a powerful persuader. By awarding her an Oscar, her peers have recognized Shirley MacLaine's superior acting ability. It was her daughter, Sachi, who observed that acting is making someone believe what you say, whether it is true or not. Can Ms. MacLaine's audience distinguish between make-believe on stage and make-believe about life and afterlife?

On talk shows, Shirley MacLaine runs on stage with an air of confidence, smiles at the camera, and launches into a power-of-positive-thinking monologue. "We need to get out of our material mindset and realize our spiritual potential through self-awareness and higher consciousness," she says. "We need to take on personal responsibility for our lives. Skepticism is a limiter, and fear is a governor. We must rid ourselves of fear." If that's where her message stopped, one could partly agree with it. But behind the scenes is a pervasive mystical philosophy which Ms. MacLaine only hints at in the limited time afforded by a brief television appearance.

In *Out on a Limb*, Ms. MacLaine weaves an intricate tapestry of seemingly unrelated ideas and phenomena—everything from death to intimate sexual relationships, from trance mediums to psychic healers, from the paranormal to the metaphysical, from reality to illusion, from Holy Scriptures to legends, and from past lives to future reincarnations. The belief system that results from this collage goes far beyond simply an enthusiastic public figure asking us to adopt a philosophy of nonjudgmental love and positive spiritual energy.

Is Shirley MacLaine dancing in the light? Or is she blinded by a floodlight of speculation in which she has indulged too long? Can the evidence she presents for reincarnation withstand cross-examination? What lessons *can* we learn from death? Is life only an illusion? Is reality only what we each perceive it to be?

Readers of Ms. MacLaine's books are urged to consider

some outrageous notions along the way to the new age of enlightenment: Does deja vu provide evidence of former lives? Do astral projections prove the soul's ability to reincarnate? Is truth conveyed to us by extraterrestrials in UFO's? There is great risk in tying one's eternal spiritual destiny to a belief system based on experiences and speculations as uncertain as Ripley's Believe-It-Or-Not.

Ms. MacLaine's personal quest has led her to spiritual mentors who claim to have a hotline to truth and omniscience. Are her mediums legitimate "human telephones" to spiritual advisers on the astral plane, or are they frauds? Do they deserve Oscars for improvisational acting, or are they themselves puppets in a demonic Punch-and-Judy show? Is Shirley "the *good* witch," as she has laughingly referred to herself, or has she actually gotten herself mixed up in witchcraft?

Reincarnation is only the enticing tip of the philosophical iceberg being towed into our lives. The danger that lies beneath the surface of Shirley MacLaine's eclectic belief system must be examined and exposed, for this is not a matter of fun and games: Eternal life and death are in the balance.

CHAPTER TWO

LESSONS FROM AN AUTOPSY

"Man is a little soul carrying around a corpse."

—EPICTETUS
Fragments

READING SHIRLEY MACLAINE'S BOOKS was not my first experience with questions of life and death. Many times in my life I had faced those questions, sometimes with the innocence and optimism of naïve youth, sometimes with struggle and questioning, sometimes with the security of the promises of God. But my greatest lesson about death came when, as a young District Attorney in Oregon, I watched an autopsy for the first time.

The morgue was cold and sterile, with antiseptic ceramic tile covering the floor and walls. With the odor of death in the room, I was thankful that the big Oregon State Police sergeant standing next to me was puffing on an old smelly cigar, despite the early hour of the morning. I was fearful of disgracing myself by either throwing up or fainting.

It never occurred to me that I could have skipped my early morning appointment with the coroner. As District Attorney in a rural eastern Oregon county, part of my responsibility was to familiarize myself with the circumstances of each criminal homicide. But nobody had told me that autopsy attendance was mandatory. I suppose I could have just read the autopsy report written by the pathologist, but an odd mixture of curiosity and eager dedication to my job had compelled me toward the morgue that morning.

In the middle of the room, occupying center stage, was the stainless steel examining table. On it lay the stiffened body of a young man, about 25 years old. He and I were the same age. Yesterday he had been alive, as I was alive now. He had felt no premonition that he was living his last day in this world. But that fateful day he had argued with his girlfriend, thrown some clothes into a suitcase, and stormed out of the house. He was just a little way down the country road when his girlfriend drove up from behind, aimed her car straight at him, and rammed him squarely in the back. The impact sent him over the hood and roof of the car before he landed hard on the road—twisted, broken, bleeding, and fatally injured.

Now he was dead. And here we were together, brought together not because of his life but because of his death. I had seen dead people before. As a youngster I had attended many funerals—some of them for elderly relatives of mine—and I had even sung hymns at funeral services. But there's a big difference between cosmetic mortuary death and the starkly brutal death I faced this day. I could see the blue fingernails, the dried blood, the partially formed bruises, the slack mouth, the barely discernible stubble shadowing the body's puffy jaw. Somehow it was easier to think of "the body" rather than "the man"—a man too much like me to allow me to be comfortable in his death. I had never touched a dead body. I wondered what it would be like.

As we waited for the pathologist to arrive, there was an air of expectancy in the room. Voices were hushed and we hardly moved. I was glued to the wall, acting as though it were my responsibility to hold it up, but knowing the truth—that it was the wall which was actually holding me up. I was as far away from the body as I could be, and I had no intention of coming closer.

Suddenly the morgue door opened and Dr. Scott entered. Briskly and professionally gathering up his macabre tools, he greeted us heartily, as if we were meeting for an Optimist Club breakfast. Murder and corpses seemed to him like nothing more than any professional's stock-in-trade.

His scalpel gleamed in the bright lights as he made the first quick incision. A quick Y-shaped cut just below the neck, a long vertical slice down to the middle of the abdomen, and the entire chest cavity blossomed into view. This was no high school biology book illustration. I was fascinated with the intricacy, the complexity, the muscles, veins, and organs. I was drawn involuntarily closer to this master machine. I wanted to see up-close the secrets of human life. Dr. Scott noted my new interest and launched into careful instruction on the basics of anatomy. He enjoyed the role of a teacher, carefully explaining the function of each organ. I was most intrigued by his explanation of where the organs were placed. The most vital ones were in the best-protected areas and the others were nestled together in close companionship in the abdomen. The words of the Bible came back to me: We are "fearfully and wonderfully made."

In order to determine the cause of death, the pathologist needed to study each organ closely. He reached to the back of the chest cavity and ran his hand behind the fleshy tissues, pulling the major organs out of the opening and laying them matter-of-factly on the still-intact abdomen. Without emotion he commented, "It's just like cleaning an elk after a good day's hunting."

And yet the comparison didn't sicken me. In fact, I

thought it appropriate. In death, there was little difference between a human body and any other body. I remembered how it was easier to call it "the body" instead of "the man." It struck me: This wasn't a man but a shell. The man was gone.

He had left his body so quickly. How fragile human life now seemed! Not only could a man be severed from his body at almost any instant, but that body itself was in an almost-constant betrayal. Almost before it matures, the body begins to deteriorate. Dr. Scott showed me the early signs of arteriosclerosis in the 25-year-old body, and I wondered if the same creeping decay was hiding in my own body. Death wasn't 50 years away anymore; it was staring me in the face. I was reminded of another Bible verse which calls our bodies the "outer man," and acknowledges that this outer man is always decaying.

But the most important lesson of the morning was yet to come. I was about to understand, for the first time, that the essence of a human is not material, but spiritual—that "me" was not equivalent to "my body." If someone had asked me before this day where my real person was physically located, I would have identified the mind or the brain (which seems to house the mind). After all, my thinking process harbors my innermost feelings.

We talk about "matters of the heart," but no one believes that love, hate, guilt, or happiness are literally found in the organ that pumps our blood. It is more a matter of having two different thinking processes—one more logical and rational and the other more emotional and intuitive, but both inseparably tied up with thinking. The brain is where we think. And are we anything without thinking? Doctors and lawyers even use terminology such as "brain death" to determine when someone is no longer alive.

Before all this philosophical analysis could filter through my mind, the pathologist made an incision just below the corpse's hairline and deflected the scalp. The most gruesome part of the autopsy was about to take place. With a small buzzing rotary saw, the pathologist quickly sawed out a large piece of the skull. To this day I remember that grating sound. Just as quickly he removed the brain.

My queasy disgust turned immediately to alert fascination as Dr. Scott carefully examined the brain, telling us finally that there appeared to be nothing wrong with it. It was a normal, healthy brain. "A normal, healthy brain?" I asked myself. "If it is in fact a normal, healthy brain—and if life is in the brain—why is he dead?"

I knew for the first time from experience what before I had believed by faith: Who I am is not limited to my body. My personality is not a by-product of my brain, to die and decay like the rest of my body. Who I am uses and expresses itself through my body, but it is more than my body. My body is only part of me—not my essential being. My emotions are not merely electrical responses to stimuli, but are more than that. When I laugh, there is more involved than just the electrical impulses of the brain telling my throat and lungs to work together to make sounds associated with laughter. When I cry, my tears are prompted by something in addition to brain waves. The trendy talk about left-side and right-side brain functions falls far short of providing any explanation of who I am. It is the *spirit* part of the brain that matters.

Every gram of physical weight which this man on the autopsy table had possessed before death still lay there in front of me. He still had every one of his organs and limbs. But *he* wasn't there. What this body was missing was not physical, not material, not quantifiable in grams and centimeters. Just a day before this body had been a *person*—with intelligence, feelings, and emotions—not just a living, breathing physical organism. Nor had this *person* been simply another animal. Animals also have intelligence, feelings, and emotions, but human beings are more than animals. Human beings have will, self-awareness, and nonmaterial aspirations, dreams, and goals. Only humans philosophize. Only humans hunger after the metaphysical. Only humans can be aware of and relate to their Creator. This corpse in front of me was a discarded, decaying shell: The person was no longer there.

I experienced a great truth that morning in Oregon: Although the human body is wonderful and the brain is a sophisticated organism, the spirit of a human being is more than one's body, and the spirit is not bound to the body in death. On the contrary, it is the spirit which gives the body life, not the body which gives the spirit life.

I'm not saying that the human body has no value—far from it. But neither should anyone be obsessed with his own body or anyone else's body. The person is more than the body. All the makeup, plastic surgery, workouts, and designer clothes will not change a person's essence. The body is a natural and necessary part of my whole being, but I am not defined by or limited to my body alone. Death pictures, as nothing else can, the fact that the spirit leaves the body at death.

Years after the autopsy experience, I remembered what I had experienced at the autopsy, and it influenced a very personal decision I had to make: whether or not to look one last time at my father's body while it was open to view at the funeral home after his death. I did not look, and I've never regretted my decision, for my father was not in that casket. My view of death had been radically altered by the autopsy experience. These new insights helped soften the blow of my father's passing. "Passing" accurately describes death. It reflects an intuitive sense of the spirit's continuity after the death of the body.

For weeks afterward, the lessons of the autopsy colored my thinking. I viewed the world around me in a new light. I concentrated on life's meaning and ultimate things. I was not obsessed with considerations about my body and the bodies around me. I saw myself and other people differently. I found myself performing "spiritual autopsies" on those I loved the most. What was it that made me love them? What was it that attracted me to them? Was it their physical bodies? Was it their minds or emotional makeup? I tried to see their inner selves, the persons they were in essence, expressed through their bodies, but not material in themselves.

If this view of life is another way of saying we ought not to look at other people merely as objects, sexual or otherwise, then I had joined the movement. We are *human beings*, and that is wonder enough. Of far greater significance—and crucial to understanding what life is all about—is the fact that we are first and foremost spiritual beings.

We rightfully give a great deal of attention to our bodies—how we dress them, feed them, exercise them, educate them, and entertain them. It is little wonder, then, that we think of ourselves primarily as physical human beings, having secondary spiritual natures we can't quantify or explain. As Aleksandr Solzhenitsyn observed, we are outraged if someone gives his soul as much daily attention as his grooming. But that's all backward. The truth is that we are primarily spiritual beings within quite secondary physical bodies.

Jesus confirmed that we are spirits when he said we are

to love God with all our heart, soul, mind, and strength—not only with our human bodies, or even our emotions or intellect, but also with our spirit selves—our souls. The apostle Paul also pointed to the soul of a person when he rhetorically asked, "Who among men knows the thoughts of a man except the man's spirit within him?" Paul made a clear distinction between man's spirit and man's brain and body.

On this point Shirley MacLaine and I agree: What we are is mind, body, *and* spirit.

But Ms. MacLaine has missed the mark. While many people focus on the material to the exclusion of the spiritual, she sometimes focuses on the spiritual close to the point of excluding the material. Either extreme is unbalanced and unrealistic. Just because we are spirit beings in a material world does not mean that the material world is not real, or that reality is only what each of us perceives it to be.

✦

ENCOUNTER IN EUROPE

An encounter I had in Europe recently made me even more aware of the problems inherent with upsetting that delicate balance. I was on my way into Switzerland from Germany, and I stopped at the Basel border crossing to change currency. In the parking lot was a young German carrying a backpack. I guessed him to be a student about 19, dressed in jeans and a dark green cloth jacket. He asked if I could give him a ride to Bern. My usual wariness about hitchhikers was overcome by the look of urgency on his face, and so I obliged.

As I turned my rented yellow Volkswagen onto the Autobahn heading south, the usual travelers' questions began. "Where are you from?" "How long have you been in Europe?" "Where are you going from here?" When it got to, "What are you doing here this summer?" I said I was writing a book. At that, Karl's eyes lit up.

"It's about life and afterlife." (How do you explain to people that you're writing a book about such simple subjects as life and death!) Karl laughed, but it was the kind of laugh that told me I had struck a responsive chord. What a coincidence, he told me. He was on his way to a "birthing session," a workshop for people wishing to "get in touch with themselves." It would involve learning how to breathe correctly, being "reborn," as it were.

"Why is that necessary?" I asked.

"We have to get out of our bodies and into our awareness," Karl replied.

"Is there something wrong with our bodies?" I countered.

"Well, they don't really exist. We just *think* they exist. The ego tells us they exist, and we need to learn to ignore that, and just focus our awareness on true reality. God is truth. God is everywhere. He is in us; he is in the trees, and in those rocks over there. And we are in God. We are one with God."

"Who created everything?" After all, I thought, how can he maintain that everything is God if God is eternal and the world around us is not, but is created?

His response was immediate: "God did."

"But if we are one with God," I tested him, "did we also create everything?"

"Yes."

"But how can we be both Creator and creature?" I really didn't understand how he could hold such inconsistent beliefs.

That seemed to stump Karl momentarily, and in silence we wound our way through tunnels and over the green carpeted fields of the uniquely beautiful Swiss countryside.

"Life is really an illusion," he started again. "We are what we *choose* to believe we are. We are responsible for everything that happens to us."

"You mean we *choose* to live?"

"Yes."

"Do we also choose to die?"

"Yes. Life lasts for as long as we choose to live. There are people who choose not to die and live to be 300 to 500 years old."

Now we were getting somewhere, I thought. Here was something we could test. "Really? Have you *seen* these people?"

"No, but I've read about them. They live in India."

("Of course they would live in India," I thought to myself.)

I genuinely liked Karl. I didn't want to drop the conversation at that point when his worldview was so far away from reality. So I persisted in our casual give-and-take. "What happens when a plane crashes? Does everyone on board *choose* to die?"

"Yes!" he said with more emphasis than necessary, as if to underscore his sincerity in the face of the incredible. "Nothing happens by accident. There are no victims."

"You mean the Ethiopians and their children are not victims? They actually *chose* to be a part of that suffering?"

His responding "of course" lacked the conviction of his earlier affirmations. "Suffering is only suffering in our minds. It is not real. It is an illusion."

"But is it just illusion when someone kills or rapes someone else?"

"Yes. If someone kills, it's not his inner will. Only his ego.

Our egos tell us we are human, not divine. We have to get rid of our egos."

What a strange twist! Karl had been manipulated by his worldview into the same dual denial I saw in Shirley MacLaine's books: By denying the reality of a material world, he was also forced to admit the infidelity of our spiritual nature, which, as he would say, wrongfully assumes a material world. Time passed quickly and the beautiful city of Bern soon appeared. We kidded each other about whether our "chance" meeting had been cosmically ordained. Karl insisted that nothing ever happens by accident, and in this case I agreed. As he got out by the side of the road and gave me a broad smile of thanks, I hoped he would not be satisfied with his untested ideas, but would keep searching until he could find a consistent worldview which embraced the material while at the same time affirmed the spiritual.

For myself, I have found that consistent worldview in the Bible and through a personal relationship with Jesus Christ. Intellectually, I have found the Bible to be objectively consistent with the laws of nature, with human conduct, and with my own rational thought processes. It matches perfectly with what I know about history, science, and archeological discoveries. Emotionally, I personally identify with the height and depth of human experience which is presented on the pages of Scripture. When Jeremiah poignantly describes the destruction of Jerusalem by the Babylonian hordes, I sadly remember times in my own life when my ideals and goals have been shattered. And when Isaiah majestically describes how those who hope in the Lord will soar on wings like eagles, I know that exhilarating feeling as well. With each success God has given me, I have soared with excitement.

Spiritually, I can see more and more that God is working

in my life; that I am almost daily gaining new insights about my life here and about what will happen to me after death; that, with all my faults, I am a better person for the Lord than I was a year ago, or ten years ago. I have a peace that comes with spiritual perspective. And I get that perspective through my personal relationship with Jesus Christ, the Prince of Peace, the source of true inner peace. By following his teaching and example, there's more direction as to what my priorities ought to be, what projects I should become involved in, what people to spend time with, how to spend my money.

While with the passing years I increasingly discover the complexity of the world around me, there's a cohesiveness to my life which simplifies and satisfies. The Christian paradigm is a comprehensive package in which all the pieces fit. I don't have to run around grabbing frenetically at first one idea, then another—at some eclectic philosophy which requires reconciling the irreconcilable. My identity is not chained to the latest fashions, crazes, or lifestyles. I don't have to make frustrating attempts to "find myself." Sadly, I didn't have the feeling that Karl had the same assurances in his own life. Too many pieces were at odds, or actually missing, in the philosophical package he was describing to me.

✦

IS LIFE ILLUSORY?

What Karl had been telling me was all too familiar. I recognized many of the same concepts from *Out on a Limb*. Shirley MacLaine's quest for understanding life had led her to seek out a number of spiritual mentors, including Kevin

Ryerson, a kind of spiritual guru and psychic medium from San Francisco who claims to be psychically in touch with various sources of cosmic truth. While in a self-induced trance, Kevin supposedly acts as an intermediary between his clients and various spirit entities, or personalities, who are said to exist out of this world on what is known as the astral plane. People ask Kevin questions, and through artificial-sounding voices Kevin gives answers from the spirits, which, he says, use him as their "instrument." The process is known as "channeling."

One of the entities which Kevin "channeled" for Ms. MacLaine's benefit was named John. (The other entity is known as Tom McPherson.) In answering Shirley's questions about life, John agreed with Karl's idea that reality is distorted by our egos:

> "If people insist upon remaining within their logical belief systems they are safe within their own perceived reality, and thus are safe within the position of power they hold, whatever that power might be. They will not change their perceptions and thus be required to change themselves or grow into an expanded awareness of themselves." "But what about the security of one's ego?" [Shirley asked.] "Most people are suffering from *altered* egos. Altered by society, by the church, and by education. Their true egos know the truth."

"Altered egos" and illusory bodies are the opposite extreme from being too materially-minded. How can anyone believe that his body exists only in his mind, when the mind itself is part of the supposedly nonexistent body?

Not all the Eastern mystics agree that the body is illusory.

In fact, the practices of transcendental meditation and yoga are based in part on the correlation between the body and the soul. To achieve spiritual enlightenment, one concentrates his psychic energy through correct *body* position and *body* breathing. Indeed, the whole New Age movement, which has as its goal the bringing about of a new age of human enlightenment through self-awareness and self-direction, is caught up in achieving superconsciousness through diet, exercise, and meditation. There is growing recognition even among New Agers that mind, body, and spirit are a unified, symbiotic whole.

Yet there is a contradiction here. While Shirley MacLaine obviously accepts the reality of her body (perhaps more consciously than most because of her career as a dancer), she nevertheless has a strong belief in the illusory nature of our perceptions. She believes that truth and reality are relative, existing only in the mind. To Ms. MacLaine, reality is what each of us decides it is.

And yet objective reality displays itself to us on a daily basis. We see it in the first cry of a newborn babe; the love in families; flowers; and fresh spring showers. There is cold reality in tyrants, toothaches, and taxes. And when earthquakes kill thousands, there is the accepted reality of real people trapped alive in real concrete rubble, and of real family members who are actually dead. Every day the entire world functions pursuant to accepted reality. Those who are found to be "out of touch with reality" are rightly regarded as mentally imbalanced.

If Ms. MacLaine were simply telling us that our misplaced emphasis on a material world has left us *spiritually* imbalanced, she would be making an important statement, one we need to hear. But in *Dancing in the Light*, she comes close to saying that spiritual consciousness is all there is. She aligns herself with those who believe that "the *cosmos* [is] nothing but consciousness. That the universe and God itself might just be one giant, collective 'thought.' " She also quotes Flaubert's statement with approval: "There is no such thing as reality. There is only perception."

✦

NO SUCH THING AS EVIL?

An important and necessary corollary to this is just as faulty: She concludes that there is no such thing as evil. Evil to her is only what you *think* it is. By that reasoning I can still choose to think that discrimination, child abuse, murder, and war are evil. But what concerns me is the implication that others can just as easily choose to think that those things are *not* evil. Such relativism justifies terrorist bombings and Nazi atrocities.

To be fair, according to Ms. MacLaine's psychic friend, Kevin, such socially irresponsible thinking would reflect spiritual ignorance on their part. But Ms. MacLaine herself insists that other people have "their own perceptions, their own truth, their own pace, and their own version of enlightenment. It [is] not possible to judge another's truth." Does that mean it was all right for Hitler to have his own truth? Was there no evil in what he did? Is it only our *personal perception* that what Hitler did was evil?

I can't agree with that. Part of what distinguishes humans from all other life forms is our conscience. Animals may be violent, but they are not capable of moral evil. People are. Unfortunately, "judging" another person's truth has become for many people, including Ms. MacLaine, the worst sin of all, which of course is itself a judgment! Is it because they believe there is no absolute truth, no center stripe down the highway of life? Or is it that they want to insulate themselves from having their wrong beliefs exposed? If one judges another's motives, or sets himself up as having superior insight which the rest of the world must follow, then that self-righteous attitude is rightly judged by others as being wrong. But who would permit a child to run in front of an oncoming car without making an effort to warn the child of the danger? There are judgments that destroy and judgments that protect.

Just because people are *unaware* of danger in their lives, whether physical or spiritual, doesn't mean that they are not in fact in danger. While passengers on board the *Titanic* were dancing in the light, death loomed just ahead in the darkness. Warning people with *Titanic* philosophies is not a matter of judgmentally questioning their sincerity or right to choose. It is telling them that what they perceive to be true may be a life-threatening misunderstanding of actual truth.

Not only does Shirley's worldview deny the absolutes of good and evil, but it also necessarily denies the existence of tragedy or sorrow. She asserts, "Tragedy is tragedy because we *perceive* it as such." Does she mean that death is not tragic? That suffering is not tragic? That broken relationships are not tragic? If all she means is that what we now consider to be tragic will ultimately appear in our life after death to be less significant, then I could agree. But Ms. MacLaine is speaking of our *present* perception when she says that tragedy is all in the mind.

THE SELF-CHOICE PREMISE

Ms. MacLaine's remarkable conclusions are based upon still

another premise, a premise I had discussed with young Karl in Europe: We *choose* what happens to us, "whether it was a love affair, a death, a lost job, or a disease. *We* choose to have these experiences in order to learn from them. . . ." A similar sentiment is expressed by est (now called The Forum), a human-potential-movement group, which maintains that everyone chooses his own experiences. This apparently means that babies in Vietnam chose to be napalmed, your friend down the street chose to be raped, and so forth. Victims vanish, to be replaced by macabre masochists! As Ms. MacLaine says, "In truth, there are no victims. There is only self-perception and self-realization."

Why is it, then, that passengers on a death flight hurriedly scribble notes to their loved ones as if they hadn't known in advance that they had chosen to take a flight on which the engines would fail? Ms. MacLaine gave us a clue when she said of a close friend who was dying of cancer: "He has to accept that he had elected to have this experience, which is not going to be pleasant." So we choose, says Ms. MacLaine, but we don't always *realize* that we are choosing. In fact, as her statement suggests, we would have to jump an incredibly high hurdle of disbelief in order to *accept* that we choose to lose our jobs, that we choose to be seriously injured in automobile accidents, that we choose to have children who are crippled at birth (while the children themselves are choosing to be born handicapped), and so on. Far from being a philosophy of happiness and fulfillment, this is an irrational belief system which robs people of self-dignity and reduces human suffering to personal whims.

Yet Ms. MacLaine offers this worldview as *fulfillment* to anyone who adopts it! According to her, we have both a higher self and a lower self. Apparently it is the higher self which cons the unwitting lower self into boarding the ill-fated plane. "Take Korean flight 007," says higher self; "it's going to be a good experience for you." So lower self obediently packs his bags, kisses his wife and children goodbye, and climbs on board, unwittingly sealing his fate at the hands of Soviet military pilots.

Incredibly, this scenario gives Shirley MacLaine great comfort. To Ms. MacLaine, there is no such thing as accident; everything that happens is the result of inexorable cause and effect: fate. "There is always a reason," she says. "We are all participants in our own karmic drama from lifetime to lifetime."

Here's where her reincarnation philosophy makes an entrance. According to Ms. MacLaine, the higher self has existed from the beginning. It has chosen to incarnate numerous times into various physical bodies on the planet earth. The purpose of these many incarnations is to learn through experience. When an entity is incarnated, it takes on a lower self which is capable of both enlightenment and ignorance. When the lower self becomes more enlightened, it evolves spiritually to a higher level of awareness. When the lower self manifests ignorance, it requires further education.

Pursuant to the law of cause and effect, a person is given the opportunity to reincarnate in order to achieve higher levels of awareness. Sometimes this requires that the lower self experience what is *perceived* as trauma and tragedy, although in the process of spiritual evolution those dreaded occurrences are really just learning experiences. If left to the lower self, those lessons might never be learned, so the higher self chooses on behalf of the lower self what it will experience on the earth-plane.

Reality, therefore, is not as it is perceived by the lower self.

There is no such thing as evil because even bad experiences are good learning experiences. There are no victims—just gods in the making. And there are no accidents, because higher self is choosing the path to enlightenment. Such a spiritual journey can be celebrated, says Ms. MacLaine, by enjoying a new age of thought and awareness, so that we can understand that there is a greater reality than our perceived reality. We need to achieve a higher consciousness, a broader consciousness, a spiritual consciousness.

THINKING COHERENTLY

Greater spiritual awareness? Yes, it's sorely needed. Broader perspective as to what life is all about? Yes, we all need help in that area, and Ms. MacLaine's spiritual emphasis is right on target for a materially minded world. Clearer understanding that this life is not our final destiny? Certainly! As Shirley says, we are in a spiritual world whether we admit it or not. But that's where Ms. MacLaine and I part company. Anyone who sees the importance of having a coherent, consistent worldview with the ability to objectively understand life must reject the premises of Ms. MacLaine's Eastern thinking.

Life is not an illusion. Truth is not relative. Reality is not simply what I perceive it to be, but is the reality of an intelligent, purposeful Creator. My God, the God of the Bible, is a loving God. He does not tease me with illusion. He does not hide truth behind doors of relativity. He does not ignore evil as if it did not exist. Nor does he sentence me to unmitigated suffering. He does not leave me to myself to achieve oneness with him through futile efforts at self-enlightenment. He does not find me lacking and repeatedly send me back into the earth-plane until I "get it right." He does not sentence me to grope for the light in the midst of darkness: He is "the light that enlightens every man coming into the world."

No, human life is not illusory. It is real and it is good. It was made for us to enjoy while we prepare ourselves spiritually for the one life to come. No one knew this better than Jesus. While he taught that we should seek first the spiritual kingdom, he did not teach that we should deny the reality of our present existence. He immersed himself in life's reality, in both its suffering and its enjoyments.

Jesus, though he was God, was God *in the flesh*, not just a spirit-being roaming about in the earth-plane. When Thomas doubted that the crucified Jesus had actually risen from the dead, Jesus proved his resurrection by pointing to the wounds in his hands where he had been nailed to the cross. It is not an illusion, Jesus was saying. Look at my physical body for the evidence!

The soul, or spirit, is real and the body is real. Body and soul are intrinsically and essentially *one*. We don't just *have* a spirit within a package; we *are* spirit. We don't just *have* a body which contains a spirit; we *are* body. And the two—body and spirit—are *one*. To dichotomize the spirit from the body before death (which separates them) is to deny the creative wisdom of God in making us body and spirit, a unified whole. To say that the body and soul are one is not to say that they are the same. The distinction is something I easily recognize within myself. My body and soul are often in conflict. I want to do what is right, but I don't always follow through. Often I do what I know I shouldn't do, and I don't do what I know I should.

But my body-soul struggle is not the same as Shirley MacLaine's higher self and lower self. As Ms. MacLaine sees it, the lower self is not naturally aware of what the higher self is perceiving or choosing to do. In her concept of the human personality, it is as if there were *two* selves, acting separately, not an inner conflict within *one* self. But I am fully aware at all times of my conflicting thoughts, desires, and actions. I am aware that one part of me wants to be spiritually-minded. At the very same time I am aware that another part of me wants to go another direction. There is an important difference between my soul and Shirley's higher self. At any given moment I know what my conscious soul is telling me, whereas Shirley has to approach her higher self, almost as a separate person, through meditation, yoga, dreams, or psychic acupuncture.

Jesus unerringly observed what many of us have said jokingly: "The spirit is willing, but the body is weak." The body in this case represents our mortal, fallen nature. It is attracted by that part of the material world which glitters like gold but which turns out to be no more than fool's gold. The soul, on the other hand, represents that part of our being which responds to the call of God, communes with the sublime, and is attracted by the spiritual, the eternal. We are *both* intellectual and intuitive, *both* physical and spiritual, *both* good and evil, *both* mortal and immortal.

There is a wonderful complexity to human beings. No single aspect of the human personality can be considered adequately without consideration of every other part. The physical cannot be emphasized without mention of the spiritual. The spiritual cannot be seen in a vacuum apart from the physical. In this life there is no essential and unfathomable abyss between our physical existence and our spiritual existence. On the contrary, the union between our physical and spiritual aspects is a creative dynamic designed and nurtured by the supreme God who created us. If you take away the reality of either mind or body or spirit from the human personality, you throw away one of the keys which unlocks the mysteries of our existence.

✦

WHY STUMBLE IN THE DARK?

As the material world exerts more and more influence over our lives, we turn almost instinctively to the mystical and the mysterious. In search of our identities we are willing to go to great lengths for an explanation, even if our search should lead us to the bizarre. And often we are not careful to sift through and test the bombardment of conflicting and competing beliefs thrust upon us for immediate consumption. We become ripe for paranormal exploitation, and it is there that Shirley MacLaine takes us—to a Twilight Zone of curiosity filled with mystics, mediums, trance-channeling, deja vu, ESP, and UFO's.

Before launching off into a world of speculation about the various strange phenomena which are said to support the notion of reincarnation, there is this to consider: UFO's are fun to talk about until they are used to support a pervasive philosophy of life. Are we willing to risk the destiny of our eternal existence on a belief in flying saucers? Deja vu is interesting and ESP is intriguing, but do they give us any assurance that we have more than one life to live? Mediums may be faddish and psychics may be the latest craze, but where are they leading us? To a meaningful life and after-life, or to spiritual disaster?

CHAPTER THREE
FASCINATION AND FANTASY

"It is never a question with any of us of faith or no faith; the question always is, 'In what or in whom do we put our faith?' "

—ANONYMOUS

THE PACKAGE OF VIEWS OFFERED by the metaphysical enchanters wouldn't be very enticing all by itself, so they sweeten the offer by responding to people's natural questioning about the mysteries which surround them in life. Extraterrestrials seem the stuff of kids' movies until we have a vivid experience with an object in the sky that we don't know how to explain. ESP seems like mental sleight of hand until we have a shocking mental communication that we can't explain. Reincarnation seems like an engaging mind game for bored philosophy students until we ponder the tough question of the suffering of "innocents." Much in our world is mysterious. We just don't know enough to satisfy our curiosity. But where those who embrace Eastern thought make a wrong turn is in thinking that *any* explanation is better than none, that any attempt to answer life's puzzles is as valid and true as any other. As a law professor, I insist that my students reject easy but shallow explanations, since truth, even difficult truth, is what really matters.

I don't mean that I necessarily reject the validity of strange experiences or perceptions; I believe that mysterious things sometimes do happen. Like many other people I know, I have had experiences which I cannot explain. For example, once when working late into the night writing a criminal law textbook, I got a call from one of my sisters who very anxiously asked if I was all right. She had just awakened from a frightening dream in which she had seen me kill myself. While committing suicide would never even cross my mind, the irony is that, at the very moment she was having the dream, I was writing the section in the book dealing with suicide! On a prior occasion, acting strictly on a hunch, I had called the same sister half a world away at a time when she desperately needed to talk to someone. Were these both a form of mental telepathy, or nothing more than coincidence? Why have there been other times when one of us has been in even tougher situations and the other one has had no inkling at all about what was going on?

Without doubt, there is a spiritual dimension to every person which people tend to ignore. If that allows for a kind of mental telepathy I can't be certain, but I do know that through my prayers I can communicate with the Creator God of the universe, and that the Holy Spirit makes that communication possible. This spiritual telepathy is one of God's best gifts to me. When something in my life needs his special touch, I am confident that he uses his supreme spiritual power in the physical world on my behalf. God has promised this in the Bible, I have seen it work in other people's lives, and I have seen it work in my own life.

The Bible is filled with examples of the spiritual dimension. Jesus was able to know the thoughts of his adversaries even before they spoke. Physical healings were often linked to one's spiritual condition or personal faith. Spiritual gifts of prophecy and interpretation allowed God's chosen prophets to foretell future events and provide the explanation for God-sent visions and dreams. Certain of God's spokesmen were caught up into a spiritual realm where they were shown otherworld scenes. Dead people were brought back to life. Angry waves were stilled by the Master's voice.

Page after page of Scripture unfolds with examples of the supernatural. Whether we have access to all of those spiritual avenues today is not always clear. But it is important for us to realize that those avenues *do exist*. The physical universe which we find ourselves in is surrounded and permeated by an even greater spiritual universe. We may not always know how it works, but we cannot deny its presence.

In recent years I have gained new appreciation for the remarkable possibilities associated with my spirit self. Nevertheless, I am baffled as to why Ms. MacLaine and others offer paranormal experiences as proof of reincarnation. Even if two people could communicate telepathically, what evidence would that be of previous or future lives? To acknowledge a spiritual dimension in *this* life says nothing about *past* lives. To be aware that we can operate on a spiritual plane in *this* life says nothing about the possibility of *future* lives. Basing our spiritual destiny on the speculative and the unknowable is not traveling on the road to enlightenment; it is just groping in the dark.

TITILLATED BY STRANGENESS

People who believe in reincarnation often find support for their belief from the occult, the paranormal, the superstitious, and the legendary. *Out on a Limb* is filled with talk of deja vu, UFO's, astral projections, and near-death visions.

Naturally, in all of this strangeness something will sound familiar to each of us. We've all experienced deja vu—the feeling that we've been in a given circumstance or environment before, and that we are reenacting a scene we've acted out at a previous time. We all seem to have a kind of "sixth sense" about certain things or certain people—an intuition beyond our normal physical senses. Most of us have had the feeling, when first introduced to certain people, that we've known them before.

Ms. MacLaine and her spiritual mentors use deja vu as "an example of previous existence," although they don't all agree as to how it works. Some believe that deja vu is the result of cellular memory, or ancestral memory, in which we inherit the prior experiences of our ancestors. Others believe that the soul projects to a future time, and then, when that time arrives, causes us to remember the prior projection. Those who are hard-core reincarnationists believe that they are reliving experiences from previous lives.

My own deja vu experiences are limited to people I have known in this life, and buildings, cars, and other physical surroundings which are clearly a part of my present life. I never see anything from another time and place. My own experience has given me no evidence of either ancestral memory or prior-life memory.

Some psychologists theorize that deja vu is the mind's convoluted recollection of a *past similar encounter*, based either on a single experience or perhaps a composite of experiences. Even Ms. MacLaine rests her case for greater self-awareness on the premise that the human mind is capable of storing volumes of information which we normally do not access. Perhaps deja vu is that rare instance when the mind *does* access the memory bank, as if intrigued by the similarity of past and present experiences.

Others theorize that deja vu is like an electrical short circuit in our brain. It's almost like a similar occurrence on television when there is a breakup in the transmission. The picture becomes a series of stop-action still pictures which have gaps between them. During those gaps the mind invariably attempts to fill in the missing pictures. That is, after all, the very way in which motion pictures are able to work: The mind fills in the gaps between the many individual still pictures.

The brain is electronic in nature, receiving and sending impulses in much the same way as a computer or a television set. The brain can also experience momentary electronic breakup. If that happens, it would not be surprising if we were to experience deja vu immediately following a gap in transmission. If we think we've previously seen what we're looking at, it's because we *have*—milliseconds before.

None of these explanations break new ground, and my ideas will not end the discussion about deja vu. However, the point is that there may be numerous reasons other than the alleged fact of reincarnation. There is simply no logical connection between deja vu and reincarnation. In fact, for reasons soon to be discussed, reincarnation is among the *least* likely explanations.

UFO'S AND ET'S

While speaking of the strange and unbelievable, it is impossible to talk about *Out on a Limb* without mentioning Shirley MacLaine's belief in UFO's and extraterrestrials. When the supposed astral-plane entity "John" was being channeled through her medium, Kevin, Ms. MacLaine asked John about that kind of phenomenon:

"And the possible extraterrestrial references in the Bible were real? I mean in Ezekiel and all that?"

"That is correct. They appeared at that time on your Earth to bring higher knowledge of God and spiritual love."

Shirley then asked Kevin himself, her spiritual mentor, what *he* thought. Did *he* believe in ET's? "Sure," he said, "why not? Not only are they mentioned all through the Bible, but they figure in one form or another in nearly every culture on Earth."

Shirley's friend, David, agreed that "they're all over the Old Testament. There are all sorts of descriptions that sound like spacecraft to me, and to many others, of course."

Ms. MacLaine then did her own reading in the Bible. This was her understanding of what happened in the parting of the Red Sea:

> In the book of Exodus a vehicle that moved and led the Hebrews out of Egypt to the Red Sea was described as "a pillar of cloud by day and a pillar of fire by night." The pillar hovered over the waters and parted them enabling the Israelites to escape into the wilderness.

But let's look at the account ourselves:

> Then the angel of God, who had been traveling in front of Israel's army, withdrew and went behind them. The pillar of cloud also moved from in front and stood behind them, coming between

the armies of Egypt and Israel. Throughout the
night the cloud brought darkness to one side and
light to the other side; so neither went near the
other all night long.
    Then Moses stretched out his hand over the sea,
and all that night the Lord drove the sea back with
a strong east wind and turned it into dry land.
The waters were divided, and the Israelites went
through the sea on dry ground, with a wall of
water on their right and on their left (Exodus
14:19-22).

There is no basis here for referring to any "vehicles" that
may have caused the parting of the waters while "hovering" over the sea. Ms. MacLaine and her friends have read
into the biblical text only what they wanted to find, totally
ignoring the natural sense and context of the passage.
    Ms. MacLaine's interpretation of Ezekiel's famous visions
of the wheels is equally inventive and finds no justification
from the passage itself. She says:

    In the book of Ezekiel in the Old Testament,
    Ezekiel described what the Earth looked like from
    great heights. He talked of what it was like to be
    lifted into a flying ship almost as though by a
    magnet. He described the back and forth move-
    ment of the vehicle as something fast as lightning.
    He referred to the commander of the craft as "The
    Lord."

A careful contextual reading of the accounts of Ezekiel's
visions, as recorded in chapters 1 and 10 of the book of
Ezekiel, shows clearly that Ezekiel was never "lifted into"

any of the wheels he saw—whether by something like a magnet or otherwise—and that Ms. MacLaine's space-age description of the visions is only fanciful fiction.

✦

OUT-OF-BODY "PROOF"?

Ms. MacLaine frequently refers to the so-called out-of-body experiences, which many people claim to have had, as "proof" of reincarnation. But such experiences, although fascinating, present no compelling reason to accept the reincarnationists' interpretation of any such phenomena. One need not question the validity of another's personal experiences in order to justify close scrutiny of the explanations or implications which may be offered as a result of those experiences. Honesty in one's experiences is not necessarily accuracy in one's conclusions.

In the first place, not all who claim out-of-body experiences agree on either the mechanics of the sensation itself or what that feeling might be saying about our physical or spiritual capabilities. Even if part of the spirit self could float momentarily outside the body self, a person still couldn't assume that his same spirit had been incarnated in many body selves prior to this life. The "here and now" proves nothing about the "there and past." Whatever else they may be, astral projections do not suggest a previous existence, any more than ventriloquism might.

The "evidence" for reincarnation provided by the many near-death experiences which have been reported must also be tested. Even if these accounts of near-death experiences are taken to be entirely accurate, which is at least questionable, the most they indicate is that there is life *after death*. There is nothing in those experiences to even suggest, and much less prove, life *before birth*. And the very fact that they are *near*-death experiences makes their contribution to the inquiry even less helpful. If they had gone so far as to be actual *after*-death experiences (experiences after the spirit leaves the mortal body permanently), we could never know what the person had really seen, since even in our age of medical marvels, dead men tell no tales.

However, there is one out-of-body experience which does give me insight: the death, burial, and resurrection of Jesus the Christ. It is not just speculation, but a matter of historical fact. It was not simply a momentary hovering or imagining of the mind, but a complete separation of body and soul. It is an out-of-body experience that none of the near-death cases can touch. None of them can lay historical claim to have been dead for three days, buried, and *then* brought back into the body!

The out-of-body death experience of Jesus Christ, together with his supernatural, God-caused, return-to-the-body resurrection, gives me assurance of my own once-for-eternity resurrection. Because God was able to raise Jesus from the dead, I have confidence that he can raise me from the dead, never more to face death. My future is not condemned to an endless chain of births and deaths in a material world; instead, Jesus Christ teaches clearly that life after death is inexorably bound up in one's relationship to God during this one lifetime. Jesus promises that those who reconcile with God in *this* lifetime inherit and experience eternal life.

✦

DEMONS AT WORK?

I'd like to suggest a sobering source for the reincarnationists' manipulation of experiences, and that source is *demonic influence.* I am impressed by the number of encounters that Jesus had with people possessed by demons. Whoever or whatever they were, they are seen all through the Gospel accounts. But did demons really exist, and do they exist today?

Looking at the many passages about demons, one is first tempted to think that the people in Jesus' day simply used the term "demon" to refer to any illness that a person might have, particularly mental or emotional illnesses. A closer look reveals, however, that Jesus often healed people of diseases without any reference to demons. He saw a distinction between mere illness and demonic power, even though that demonic power was often manifested in physical afflictions. In healing people of deafness, muteness, or epilepsy, Jesus often rebuked a demon within the person being healed and commanded that it literally come out of the affected person. To Jesus, demons were not figures of speech to describe unknown physical conditions: They were alive and real.

In most cases, the rebuked demon would throw down the body which it had possessed and come out with a shriek! Demons were clearly individual personalities quite apart from the physical impediments they often caused in those whom they possessed. They were evil spirits who had the ability to think and speak, and they invariably recognized Jesus for who he was—the Son of God.

Several demons often joined together to possess a person. For example, Jesus cast out seven spirits from Mary Magdalene. On at least one occasion, a number of demons whom Jesus had cast out of a man entered into a herd of pigs, driving them crazy enough to run into a lake and drown.

It is not easy to understand the nature of demons, but it appears that Jesus made a connection between the demons and Satan. Once, when asked about his disciples' power over demons, Jesus told them about having seen Satan fall like lightning from heaven. It was as if he were saying that demons, like Satan, were rebellious angelic beings who came to earth to do the work of Satan.

Did demons exist only during Jesus' day in order to challenge his spiritual authority on earth? Or are they still at work in the twentieth century? Certainly they were active in the first century, even after Jesus' death. Paul, for example, cast out an evil spirit of a young girl whose power of fortune-telling was being used by some men for the profit they could make.

Even today there are fortune-tellers, just like the ones the Bible identifies as co-workers with demons, and these are not just gypsies in traveling shows. Today we call them mediums. They are quite acceptable—even fashionable. They specialize in "trance channeling." In ancient times they would have been known as witches, holding seances with the dead. In modern-day Southern California, and in Stockholm, Sweden (as Ms. MacLaine reported in *Out on a Limb*), mediums act as go-betweens for those wishing to contact otherworld spiritual guides (although nothing is offered as proof that these mediums can really deliver on their promises).

Ms. MacLaine described what she observed of an otherworld entity known as Ambres, who was supposedly channeled through a man named Sture in Stockholm, Sweden. Then, at the urging of her friends, Ms. MacLaine contacted Kevin Ryerson. It was Kevin who introduced Ms. MacLaine to several so-called spiritual guides from the astral-plane while he was in a trance in her Malibu home. Ms. MacLaine's conversations with both Kevin and the entities which he channeled ranged from theology, church history, paranormal phenomena, and extraterrestrials to reincarnation and Ms. MacLaine's supposed previous lives. Never was the word of the spirit doubted or challenged. It was as though *anything* from the spiritual dimension was necessarily good and all-knowing.

Modern mediums do not claim to directly contact the spirits of the dead. They prefer friendly spirit guides—entities who are supposedly disembodied spirits on the astral-plane. The entities allegedly have lived on the earth-plane through numerous lifetimes in various bodies, and are at various stages in their spiritual evolution. Almost always, of course, they are highly evolved spiritual beings and are therefore in a position to tutor those less highly evolved and currently incarnated on the earth-plane—you and me and Ms. MacLaine.

In attempting to learn more about MacLaine's mentor, Kevin Ryerson, I read with interest his letter of introduction to prospective clients. In the letter, Ryerson describes his work as being in the tradition of Edgar Cayce (pronounced kay-see), whose thousands of psychic readings in the first half of this century have provided an unparalleled abundance of information for Western-style reincarnationists. Unlike Kevin, however, Cayce never made use of channeled entities, but claimed only his own psychic power. The scope of Kevin Ryerson's psychic abilities is further outlined in the letter:

Trance channeling is primarily an information source. The source of this information is a vast reservoir of knowledge called the Universal Mind or the Akaschic Records. The Universal Mind is comparable to C. G. Jung's theory of the collective unconsciousness. Mr. Jung states in this theory that all of mankind's evolved higher systems of thought (i.e., Art, Philosophies, Technology, etc.) survive throughout all time and space. In a state of altered consciousness Kevin is able to tap into the vast reservoir of the Universal Mind. Subject materials as diverse as natural health therapies, the laws of physics, career direction to more esoteric subjects like Atlantis and reincarnation are expounded upon by the levels of intelligence to flow through Kevin while he is in the channeling state.

One does have to be somewhat skeptical about having access to the "Universal Mind" through someone who is half-asleep in your living room! Even Shirley MacLaine questioned it when she was first told. Ms. MacLaine's friend, Cat, at the Ashram in Calabasas (just a short drive from Malibu through the canyon), told her about trance mediums.

"What do you think would happen?" [Shirley asked.] "Oh," said Cat, "several entities come through as a rule, and it's just as though they're right in the room with you." "And what do I do?" [asked Shirley]. "Just ask anything you want. They can tell you about your past lives, or help with physical diagnosis and pain, or with diets that are good for your vibrations—anything you want...."

Ms. MacLaine remembered that Ambres had answered questions about the beginning of creation. "He described the first stirrings of God's thought and the creation of matter. He described the birth of worlds, and worlds within worlds; and universes and universes within universes."
Both Cat's recommendation to Ms. MacLaine and Kevin's

introductory letter sound very much like *omniscience at one's fingertip.* It does sound too good to be true, doesn't it? Can mediums tell me where my father is at this moment? Can they tell me when and how I will die? Can they tell me every detail of my life—all the memories of my childhood which I've forgotten and would love to remember again?

If mediums' vibrations reach back *before* creation, and if they can tell me about past lives, they should be able to tell me everything else. They should also be able to tell me things that only I am aware of. The prophets in the Bible, through whom God spoke, not only interpreted dreams related to them but could describe a dream accurately even before the dreamer told them about it!

When I attended one of Kevin Ryerson's Intuition Seminars recently, he "entered the trance state," having invited those of us present to ask him the meaning of any dreams we may have had. One woman had particular difficulty explaining her dream, and Kevin (or "Tom McPherson," the entity with whom the conversation was supposedly taking place) had to repeatedly ask for more details. I later asked "Tom" how he was able to draw from the Universal Mind in order to explain the meaning of our dreams but was unable to tell us the *dream itself.* His convenient explanation was unconvincing:

> To try and extrapolate the whole dream does two things. One, it robs a person of much of the feeling if I do it for them; and secondarily it detaches a person...if they do not go through the feeling of verbal description, they may not connect with the analysis...because the analysis must coordinate with the feelings of a person. And thus it fatigues

the "instrument" (meaning Kevin) to extrapolate all the information. And some information is wiser not to divulge. . . it may upset the emotional apple-cart.

The truth is that no psychic has the ability to tell us what dreams we may have had. And if all they can tell us is their *interpretation* of our dreams, then that interpretation is as easily invented as spiritually derived. This may explain something about why I was given one interpretation of a dream (an actual dream) which I disclosed to Kevin at the Intuition Seminar and why at a personal channeling session with Kevin four months later I received a different interpretation for the exact same dream!

But don't mediums sometimes tell you amazing things about yourself that no one else could know? Ms. MacLaine herself was startled several times when Kevin's entities seemed to know personal, undisclosed information about her. What could explain this phenomenon?

We may never know for sure. I hold strongly to the vague-pronouncements-and-coincidence theory, which explains the occasional accuracy of horoscopes and fortune cookies. However, another quite real possibility is that people who believe in trance channeling of astral entities are being spiritually deceived. Evil spirits may actually be involved.

TESTING THE SPIRITS

When dealing with the metaphysical realm of spirits, we must admit the possibility of both good spirits and evil spirits. Mediums often quote the Bible, but there is one passage which I have never seen them quote. In his first letter, the apostle John warned: "Do not believe every spirit, but test the spirits to see whether they are from God, because many false prophets have gone out into the world." This passage doesn't make headlines among today's popular mediums, perhaps because it calls on us to make spiritual judgments, the kind of judgments which Ms. MacLaine says we should not make.

The apostle John then proceeded to give a test which can be used to distinguish good spirits from evil spirits: "This is how you can recognize the Spirit of God: Every spirit that acknowledges that Jesus Christ has come in the flesh is from God, but every spirit that does not acknowledge Jesus is not from God."

Ms. MacLaine's spiritual mentors and guides acknowledge that Jesus lived in the flesh as a historical human personality, but they do not acknowledge his unique deity as *Christ*—that is, as Messiah, Savior, and only Son of God. The application of the legitimate-spirits test in this case is all too clear.

The apostle Paul also believed in the world of evil spirits. In fact, Paul saw two worlds in a cosmic battle for supremacy. He urged Christians in the city of Ephesus to "be strong in the Lord and in his mighty power. Put on the full armor of God so that you can take your stand against the devil's schemes. For our struggle is not against flesh and blood, but against the rulers, against the authorities, against the powers of this dark world and against the spiritual forces of evil in the heavenly realms."

Spirit beings may be trying to deceive us by making us think that, if we put a medium in our purse or pocket, we have ready access to some Universal Mind, as if it were a 24-hour-banking machine. Evil spirits might have access to just enough cosmic knowledge to tease us with the paranormal and with legends, superstitions, and wonderful bits of information about a host of inconsequential matters in our lives—yet provide misleading and spiritually deadly answers to our spiritual needs.

Kevin admitted to Ms. MacLaine that the Bible forbids the use of mediums, but casually tossed the biblical prohibitions over his shoulder as a self-serving part of Christian teaching against reincarnation. Actually, even the Old Testament Scriptures place mediums in bad company.

> Let no one be found among you who sacrifices his son or daughter in the fire, who practices divination or sorcery, interprets omens, engages in witchcraft, or casts spells, or who is a medium or spiritist or who consults the dead (Deuteronomy 18:10,11).

If the connection between those various practices seems strained, it's not. What they all have in common is the effort to achieve spiritual perfection through some means other than the one true God who has revealed himself and truth—uniquely in Jesus Christ and the teachings of the Bible. If truth is revealed exclusively in Jesus Christ, then an appeal to any other spiritual source can only be self-induced spiritual sabotage, resulting in an unfulfilled life and eternal separation from God.

Mediums are prohibited by Scripture not because there are no spirits who are able to invade the earth-plane but because there *are* spirits out there who are more than willing to invade the earth-plane in order to deceive us about our origin, purpose, and destiny. They are not the spirits of our dearly departed. They are spirits who are in open rebellion to God. When we deal with mediums, ancient or modern, we are seeking wisdom from the wrong source. When we deal with mediums, we are not assured of getting the right spiritual formula for our happiness, growth, and ultimate destiny. God wants us to come to *him* and to his revealed Word so that we can be assured of knowing the truth that sets us free.

Modern mediums would probably laugh at the suggestion that they are engaged in witchcraft. Fashionable Southern Californians would protest that it's not witchery to consult their clairvoyants, astrologers, healers, metaphysical counselors, and mediums with their friendly "entities." And sometimes I partly believe them. Sometimes I wonder if people in America's leisure set aren't simply playing mind games for the terminally bored. The advertising flyer for psychic Ruth Maybruck quotes actress Cloris Leechman [sic] as writing, "Ruth—your astute reading was absolutely, amazingly accurate. Also you are fun! Spending two hours with you is a pleasure." And "Sandy" writes, "The people who come to my parties can't wait for your readings. They're always asking, 'When's the next one?' "

Fun? Parties? Is that what this business of psychics is all about? If it were nothing more than fun and games, then no one would care what people do with their time and money. But there is a serious risk in this game-playing. For those who take psychics and mediums seriously—and there are a lot of people who do—it's not a matter of optional theology or mere lifestyle choices. They are becoming involved in a world of evil and ultimately in the whole realm of Satan's jurisdiction.

No one can say categorically that every medium is an instrument of Satan, nor that the entities which they claim to channel are always demonic. (Kevin Ryerson's "entities" made me want to laugh more than shudder.) Many mediums are just experts at imagination and inventiveness, seeking out the gullible in order to line their pocketbooks or satisfy their egos. But whether they intend to or not, mediums are doing the devil's work.

CHAPTER FOUR

PROVIDENCE AND PERSPECTIVE

"The longer I live, the more faith I have in Providence, and the less faith in my interpretation of Providence."

—JEREMIAH DAY

I READ WITH GREAT INTEREST the account of Shirley MacLaine's growing awareness that she was going to write *Out on a Limb*. The feeling came to her slowly but undeniably. At one point she was "a ball of vibrating confusion," wondering about herself whether "maybe the purpose of this particular collection of atoms writhing around here on the bed was to convey the message...."

Ms. MacLaine relates throughout her book the many conversations she had with her friend, David, who became one of her spiritual mentors. They shared books, yoga classes, walks on the beach, and juicy peaches, while David gradually brought Ms. MacLaine to a belief in reincarnation, UFO's, and extraterrestrials. David invited Shirley to the Peruvian Andes, where they took long mountain walks, bubbling hot baths, and wild flights of imagination. During that time David pointed Shirley to her mission, should she choose to accept it. Or did she have a choice?

"What it comes down to, Shirley, is that you're to

be a teacher. Like me. But on a much wider scale."
"A wider scale?" "Yes." "What do you mean?
I'm no teacher. I haven't got the patience. I'm a
learner." "Yes, but you like to write, don't you?"
"Oh my God," I thought. "Am I *supposed* to write
a book about all of this? Did I subconsciously plan
to do that? Was that why I took my tape recorder
with me everywhere and wrote notes at the end
of every day?"

Is Shirley MacLaine telling us that she was somehow destined or ordained by something or someone in the astral plane to write *Out on a Limb*? David said that his friend, Mayan, an extraterrestrial woman from the cluster of stars known as the Pleiades, thought that, with Shirley's "particular mental bent," Shirley "could write a very entertaining, informative account of [her] personal excursion into these matters and maybe teach people at the same time."

ᴋ

MY OWN MISSION

I think I know the feeling of being given a mission. Several years ago I began work on a chronological arrangement of the Bible. I am confident that I would never have begun or completed it without the drive of a force greater than myself. And, like Ms. MacLaine, I know that I was not the most likely candidate for the job. But as I look back, I can see the pieces of the puzzle falling together.

When I was a teenager, my father, who was a minister, sowed a seed that didn't bear fruit until 25 years later. As we walked across the parking lot after our worship one

Sunday he said simply, "Somebody ought to put the Bible in the right order." That's all I remember about the conversation, and I don't recall any further discussion about his idea.

What Dad meant was certainly no mystery to me. I knew the difficulty that most people have when they read the Bible. Unless you have a good grasp of ancient history, culture, and chronological sequence, the Bible can be somewhat bewildering.

Many years later a close friend of mine was determined to read the Bible from cover to cover. She had little background in the Bible, and reading it became difficult. During her patient struggle to sort it out, Dad's idea came back to me: "Someone ought to put the Bible in the right order." Dad was right—someone ought to do it. In fact, I wished I had a Bible like that!

After six years and hundreds of hours of work, I finally stood in Grand Rapids, Michigan, watching the first run of *The Narrated Bible* come off the press.

Working on the project was a great learning experience for me as I dug into the Bible. First of all, I was reassured to find no biblical contradictions, contrary to what I had so often heard alleged. What I found was an incredible harmony in the account of God's dealings with the human race from the beginning of time. The way God worked through nations and individuals to accomplish his will for the world impressed me. It convinced me that God had not stopped in the first century, but was working out his will even today. I was brought face-to-face with the dynamic God who loved, cared for, and actually interacted with his people.

Along the way, the project took many interesting twists and turns. When I came to the laws of Moses, I had the irresistible impulse of a law professor to take the various laws of Moses and bring them together in a unified legal code by subject matter. I also arranged the psalms into various thematic groupings and presented the 600 or so proverbs by topic. For the history of the kings, I consolidated the parallel passages and then inserted the prophets into that historical record at the time when they actually prophesied.

In the New Testament, I gathered the four Gospel accounts into one chronologically arranged account. And I inserted Paul's letters into the events recorded in the book of Acts. Seeing the need to tie together the rearranged Scripture text, I provided brief explanatory narration at the beginning of each section of Scripture. That narration eventually gave the book its name.

Was God working in the production of *The Narrated Bible*? I know that, if left solely to my own initiative, the book would not have been written. In many respects, it made no sense for me, since there are so many Bible scholars who would have been a more likely choice as author.

Yet writing the book was like piecing together the evidence for a case, as I had done so often as a District Attorney. As a teacher, what I do most for my students is to organize, synthesize, and simplify. That's what was needed for this project.

Several years ago my present editor, Eileen, had been admitted to the law school where I teach. Shortly before the fall semester started, she was asked to join the staff at Harvest House Publishers. As it turned out, instead of being one of my students, she became an indispensable colleague in the production of the book. Was God working behind the scenes in Eileen's life in order to involve her in the project?

Two more factors about my life had a direct bearing on my writing *The Narrated Bible*. The first involved a young woman whom I once thought I would marry. Through an incredible series of circumstances, she met and married someone else. As it turned out, I never married. And in retrospect I can see many ways that God has used my singleness in his work, including the freedom I had to work on *The Narrated Bible*.

The second event which I believe may have been a part of God's providence in my life was my father's death. It is not unusual that a man should die of a heart attack at the age of 63. But I am confident that his book would never have been written if he had not died. I believe that one phase of Dad's ministry may have had to end in order for the next phase to begin.

✦

OPEN TO THE TRUTH

We may be used in ways we would never have expected by either good or evil spirits—by either God or Satan. We must be open to the possibility that God may use us to achieve his ultimate good, just as we must be open to the reality that Satan really is working to gain control of this world. Yet God already has control and is working all the harder to show us the truth about who we are and what we are all about. God did not create the world only to sit back as a passive observer and watch while generation after generation of human beings come and go on the earth. As recorded in the Old Testament, God used holy men and prophets to show the way. He gave laws which guide a person safely through life. He showed the world his power and love. When entire nations disobeyed his will, he disciplined them to bring them back. When mankind's blundering attempts at moral goodness failed, he showed mercy and grace.

As if that were not enough, the New Testament tells us that God sent his only Son into the world to live an exemplary life (as a pattern for our own fulfilled living) and to die a sacrificial death to atone for our sins. The kind of "at-one-ment" with God which Shirley MacLaine and her friends talk about is mere agreement of purpose and outlook with what they *think* God holds. It is a poor imitation of the effectual atonement of Jesus' death on the cross, which expresses the great truth that God loves us, which pays the debt of our sins, and which paves the way for our eternal salvation when we choose to participate in his death, burial, and resurrection through personal commitment to Christ.

Even today, God is still working in the world and in my life and yours. He is not simply a God found in dusty books of ancient literature—he is alive and active. He shows himself in the miracle of each new birth. His name is on the pleading lips of those who suffer and in the thankful hearts of those who appreciate the quiet, unfolding beauty of a new day. In my life, God is with me in the car when I try to sort out the many pressures of my work or personal relationships which get twisted and tangled. He is with me in the morning when I plan the busy activities of the day ahead. I talk to God as I would my best friend. In fact, that is exactly who he is—my best Friend. And what he tells me through his written Word and the personal example of Jesus Christ is the kind of information I can't get from academic textbooks, encyclopedias, stock market reports, gurus, mantras, or meditation. It is truly divine insight.

In thinking about how God may be working in our lives, whether directly or more indirectly through revelation, it is important to remember that God's instruction is not a secret philosophy to which only the initiate are privy—a "hidden wisdom," as Eastern mysticism is referred to by its proponents. By inspiration, God has preserved a written record of his divine truth. Unlike the Akashic Records, which are said to contain the Universal Mind (but which only a few mystics and mediums are privileged to perceive), the biblical record is in every bookstore and hotel room for the rest of us to read.

As we turn our attention to the heart of Shirley MacLaine's philosophy—reincarnation—we must stop to consider the threshold questions about her mission. Was Shirley MacLaine *supposed* to write her books, as she suggests? If so, who sent her on that mission, and who is determining the content of her message? Is someone really pulling cosmic strings so that Ms. MacLaine can become our spiritual teacher? If so, who is pulling the strings, and what could be their purpose in trying to win us over to so dangerous a belief system?

CHAPTER FIVE

REINCARNATION, WESTERN-STYLE

"Christianity is not a theory or speculation, but a life; not a philosophy of life, but a living presence."

—SAMUEL TAYLOR COLERIDGE

WHERE DOES ONE BEGIN in sorting out the idea of reincarnation? The problem is: *whose version?* Even Shirley MacLaine's view of reincarnation is a rather eclectic version. Reincarnation is presented in many different forms, but the most basic teaching is that each soul is immortal, having always existed from the very beginning, whatever one's concept of "beginning" might be. Christians also believe that their souls are immortal, but only in a futuristic sense. For Christians, the soul does not exist before the physical body comes into being.

Among reincarnationists, some believe in an original creation of all souls by an eternally existent God-Force. Others believe in the soul's *own* eternal preexistence, involving no point in time at which there was anything that could be called "a beginning." Most reincarnationists agree that the soul is in some way a participant in the divine, all-pervading essence of God. In other words, the soul is part of God.

Whatever and whenever the soul's origin, reincarnationists believe that the soul evolves from a lower spiritual state to a higher spiritual state. It is not clear why the soul begins at such a low state of spiritual development nor even where the concept of "development" originated.

In the process of that upward evolution, the soul enters, or *incarnates*, a series of different bodies. Some—in keeping with the Hindu tradition—say that the soul gets a completely new body with each incarnation, while others—more in the Buddhist tradition—say that each new body is really the same "essence of goo" (a somewhat loose translation of the sanskrit *skandhas*) as both the soul itself and all previous bodies are composed of. Although it is not entirely clear from either of her books, it seems that Ms. MacLaine leans toward the Buddhist view. Without referring to the composition of bodies, in *Out on a Limb* she does say that *souls* are invisible entities in harmony with nature and that "none of it ever dies; it just changes form."

The early reincarnationists, and still the majority of all present-day reincarnationists, believe that the soul also incarnates into nonhuman forms, such as rocks, frogs, or trees. However, almost all Western-style reincarnationists, including Shirley MacLaine, reject the transmigration of souls from one form of life to another. In keeping with the theory of biological evolution, Western reincarnationists say that the human soul has progressed beyond the stage of such lower-life incarnations. Therefore, for them, reincarnation is limited to human bodies.

THE KARMA CONNECTION

Reincarnation must be understood as a necessary appendage to the doctrine of karma. Were it not for that doctrine, the idea of reincarnation would have no foundation upon which to rest.

The doctrine of karma teaches that each soul is working its way to perfection by overcoming imperfections in previous lives. Based upon the clearly accurate observation that no one in this present life is perfect, it is correctly assumed that a person cannot, on his own, reach perfection in a single lifetime. The fallacious conclusion is then drawn that it must take many lifetimes in order for each soul to achieve that goal.

Reincarnation is to karma what billions of years are to the theory of evolution. It makes possible a theory (perfection over many lifetimes) which, but for the additional time, would be an impossibility (self-achieved moral perfection in one lifetime).

Karma also assumes that perfection is the desired goal and necessary achievement of the human soul. Implied in this concept is a belief (not well-explained) that the soul is a fallen soul which must work its way out of its fallen state in order to achieve its original oneness with either its Creator or the Universal Soul of the cosmos.

Karma is also known as the law of cause and effect, to which Ms. MacLaine so frequently refers. She assumes that the physical laws of cause and effect are equally applicable to human behavior and moral justification. That assumption, taken together with the observable fact that no one is perfect, results in the conclusion that we keep "meeting ourselves." This karmic term means that we must face the consequences of the bad karma in our former lives. Because each of us is less than perfect, there is always a substantial amount of bad karma to account for. Although Ms. MacLaine insists that cause-and-effect is not punitive, inherent within the ideas of karma and reincarnation is the assumption that there is always karmic debt to be paid in the present life. One's good karma from former lives can build up credits toward paying off the karmic debt, but few, if any, people so far have reached that level of karmic perfection.

This brings us full circle to the doctrine of reincarnation. Because balancing good karma and bad karma is so difficult, and because we can't possibly pay off our karmic debt in one lifetime, we must live many lives—perhaps thirty, fifty, a hundred, or even thousands—in order to "get it right."

The final state of a person who eventually does "get it right" is also the subject of controversy among reincarnationists. Ms. MacLaine herself doesn't shed much light on the ultimate destiny of one who might become fully enlightened. Some believe that the soul ends up in a cosmic oneness, a kind of divine, all-encompassing spiritual soup. Some use the word "nirvana" to describe such a state of eternal existence. For them, the ultimate desirability is *absorption* into the cosmic ether, no longer enduring karma's wheel of suffering. On the other hand, many see nirvana as eternal *extinction*, not simply absorption of one's individual personality.

The modern, Westernized version of reincarnation, and perhaps the best statement of Shirley MacLaine's view, seems to focus on a perfected person ultimately becoming one with the universe. However, the significance of such an achievement is questionable because reincarnationists often insist that we were one with all things in the beginning, and that even now we are one!

GOING BACKWARD

One of the most downplayed features of Hinduism is the

possibility of going backward—devolving, so to speak. Just as one may evolve to a higher state of spiritual existence, the Hindus believe that one may also be ordered to return to a lower state, even being required to reincarnate as a plant or an animal. That would happen, for example, if one were greatly irresponsible in this life. In other words, a truly despicable person might appear someday in your grandchild's backyard as a black widow spider. This feature doesn't play well to Western audiences and is often cast off by Westerners as a cultural casualty.

There is one spin-off Hindu doctrine that is completely swept under the rug when Westerners are invited into the religious hospitality of the East. The caste system, although outlawed by the state, is still a permanent fixture in India. When it comes to human oppression, this system of rigid hierarchical social classes, with its inherent prejudice and patent injustice, blatantly discriminates against people solely on the basis of their birth.

The caste system is a natural implication of the law of karma. One's spirit-evolution stage is ascertained by looking at one's family station at birth. Since one's evolution depends on the amount of his karmic debt, one born into a less-favored caste deserves to suffer in that class as a direct result of his karmic position. If Westerners could even conceive of what it would be like to be reincarnated as an "untouchable" in India, we would never hear another word in support of reincarnation. If there really is such a wheel of reincarnation, then humankind is no better off than mindless gerbils on a treadwheel. If the reincarnation wheel actually exists, the future is not bright, optimistic, and exciting. It is bleak, pessimistic, and depressing.

Why, then, do affluent Westerners so readily turn to a teaching about life that for centuries has proved to be a trap of despair for half the world's population? While Westerners are rushing headlong into believing that reincarnation will bring about a new age of human enlightenment, those who see themselves as victims of reincarnation's vicious cycle are saying, "You're welcome to it. You can have it!"

I wonder if the answer to that mystery might not be the very fact of our Western affluence. If karma and reincarnation are an attempt to explain suffering, they are based upon a condition to which we can't even relate. We don't have any idea what real suffering is like. Instead, we pat ourselves on the back, pointing to our luxuries and material wealth as evidence of divine favor, karmic applause, and spiritual superiority. Our perspective is that of the Hindu Brahmins. We are members of the world's highest caste, and so, like them, it is easy for us to see "the wheel of suffering" as a "wheel of fortune" instead. Like the Brahmins, we can literally afford the luxury of believing in reincarnation as an idealistic theory.

To those who live in cultures dominated by a belief in karma and reincarnation, the perspective is radically different from our own. Seen through their hopeless eyes, reincarnation is not a way to freedom but a global hostage crisis.

THE TRAGIC RESULTS

The greatest embarrassment to reincarnationists is India, the birthplace of reincarnation about 3000 years ago. Pro-reincarnation literature is naturally defensive about any mention of the inhuman conditions which have existed there for centuries. It points to the insufferable climate, the uncontrollable population growth, and so on. But much of the suffering in India is directly traceable to the Hindu belief system, and more particularly to the effects of belief in karma and reincarnation.

I had the opportunity to see these effects firsthand. I remember stepping off the plane in Bombay. Even at 3:00 A.M., the sweltering heat wilted both my body and my spirit. The hundreds of people who greeted the arriving passengers were a sad-looking lot indeed. Once inside the crowded airport terminal I could hardly breathe because of the stench of human bodies, and the aroma of marijuana hung in the waiting rooms like the humidity in the air.

The early-morning darkness only partially concealed the dusty streets and dingy makeshift dwellings which I would become accustomed to seeing by day. At least I was spared the shock until I could get some rest. It's been described before, but you cannot really appreciate it fully without being there yourself. Television travelogues concentrate on the romantic highlights; rarely do they show the extent of the misery. In most places, the streets of India are appalling. While there are beautiful parts of the country itself, the human condition casts such a visual, odorous tint to the picture that, as you remember it, you wish for a karmic "veil of forgetfulness."

I have not yet forgotten the beggars, the filthy holy men, the gauze masks over the mouths and noses of the Jains to prevent their inhaling insects that might be their grand-mother, the cardboard shanties set up on the dirt sidewalks, the sacred cows wandering everywhere, the thousands of gods and gurus, the burning fires where the dead are cremated, the people bathing in the polluted Ganges River, and the children—many of them dirty, naked, and hopeless.

India is not the only suffering society—it is simply one

of the worst ones. And the excuses given for its conditions fail. A visit to China will convince you that having millions of people packed together doesn't mean that nationwide filth, begging, and lethargy are inevitable.

The Hindu culture, based in large part on the teachings of karma and reincarnation, is not a culture to be envied or admired. Its religious teachings do not lead to the New Age of enlightenment; they lead to oppression, suffering, and spiritual as well as physical death.

Anyone seriously looking for answers must ask, in the words of the law of karma, "Is there no cause and effect in what one sees in India?" Ideas have consequences too. Even if the widespread belief in reincarnation is not the only cause of the abominable living conditions in India, there is no evidence that reincarnation has done anything to help alleviate the misery.

The issue of India is acute because it is the country whose people claim centuries of access to the "hidden wisdom" of mankind's evolution to enlightenment. If they have been the trustees of true cosmic insight, why has there been no positive impact on their society? Why does India lag behind other cultures instead of showing the way?

The answer is obvious: They don't have a corner on cosmic truth after all.

✤

BORN AGAIN . . . AND AGAIN?

Reincarnation, as it has been altered by Western thinking, has become a complex and convoluted maze, added to here and there by every new "guru" of past lives. One of the most influential of those gurus was a man of visions, the late Edgar Cayce, who spent over 15 years in Virginia Beach delving psychically into reincarnation. Today Virginia Beach is the headquarters of the Association for Research and Enlightenment, which continues to promulgate reincarnation teachings based upon his thousands of "life readings."

It was important for its proponents to update *classical* reincarnation to *American-style* reincarnation (which is not found anywhere in the Hindu's sacred writings, the Vedas, to which Ms. MacLaine often refers). New Age reincarnation is distinctly Western, and with great effort is made to look as if it were compatible with Christianity.

One of the best examples of the Cayce-style reincarnation in vogue in America today is presented by John Van Auken, a lecturer for the Cayce organization, in his recent book *BORN AGAIN...and Again.*

Van Auken's explanation of life's meaning is fanciful. A composite of his imaginative reincarnation story gives a good idea of the revised reincarnationists' view of creation, man's fall, and his ultimate salvation. It is consistent with the view which Shirley MacLaine is promoting (which is drawn from the Cayce readings in which Ms. MacLaine and her medium, Kevin Ryerson, place so much credence).

Before the beginning, according to Van Auken, the consciousness of the Creator stirred itself to express thoughts, images, light, and sound. Light, stars, and galaxies then appeared, but only as an *idea*, not in physical form. According to the Secret Teachings, which manifest themselves in Cayce's readings, the Creator wanted to share this new expression of life. The Creator, therefore, conceived of individual points of consciousness like itself, companions able to perceive, conceive, express themselves, and remember.

The plan had one drawback: If the companions were to be like the Creator, they must have the freedom to *choose* to be so. And that permitted the possibility of rebellion. In order to deal with such a possibility, a Universal Law was set: For every free-willed action of a companion there would be a similar reaction or consequence upon that companion. Thereby each companion would be responsible for his use of consciousness and free will. (In other words, the Creator established the law of karma, or cause and effect.)

The creation of the companions then took place, and they thereafter went throughout the universe. In their cosmic travels, some of the companions came down into the third-dimensional influences of the planet Earth. (Van Auken does not mention how Earth came into existence, nor why it was three-dimensional.)

These entities began to think of themselves as physical entitites and soon decided that they were no longer even celestial beings, but terrestrial only. As a result, they became subject to the laws of nature. (Again, he gives no explanation of the origin of the laws of nature.)

The earth-plane entities also became subject to death. If they thought they were only physical bodies (rather than spiritual souls), then when their bodies died they assumed that *they* died. Life for them had become only biological and physical. The more they acted in the earth, the more earth debts (bad karma) they had to pay through pain, disease, loneliness, and death.

Given enough time, the earthbound creatures could become aware again of the difference between terrestrial and celestial life and realize that they were *co-creators* with the Creator of the universe, with whom they had been in the beginning. (Van Auken does not explain how something which is created can become its own creator. Others attempt the explanation that souls were always part of the Creator's eternal consciousness but that their individual beings were created from the Creator's substance.)

To help them regain a proper awareness of their celestial selves, some of the souls who had never entered the earth-plane came to the rescue. Van Auken's own words must be used at this point:

> To protect against the loss of the truth com-
> pletely, the rescuing souls wove the truth about
> the companions and their predicament into the
> fabric of physical life, into its legends and myths,
> its art and symbols. Then, when any lost soul
> sought beyond what he found in physical life,
> the real truth would be there for him. Three
> famous examples of these secret-meaning tales are
> Sleeping Beauty, Snow White and Pinocchio. . . .
> Another is the Wizard of Oz.

Van Auken's next ideas are even more incredible. He says that, because no human forms were available on the earth when the first entities came to the planet, they had to mani-fest into the animals that were already here:

> The strange creatures that remain in our legends
> today were the results of this forceful entry into
> the early earth: satyrs (beings that were half goat
> and half man), centaurs (half horse and half man),
> dryads (women living in trees, and often an entire
> "enchanted" forest of them), sphinxes (half man
> and half lion, ram or hawk; also a winged lion
> with a woman's head and breasts), and the mer-
> maids and mermen.

Don't forget that this tale is drawn from the omniscient Akashic Records (psychic data banks of cosmic history) as read by the celebrated psychic Edgar Cayce, with whose teaching Ms. MacLaine is so impressed. However, Ms. MacLaine did not choose to share these particular Cayce excerpts with her readers.

Cayce's readings indicate that at this point the Creator stepped in and used his unique power so that the companions could become human. (The obvious conflict which arises when the Creator tries to help his companions overcome their illusion of a physical world by giving them physical bodies is not addressed by Van Auken.)

Yet, because of the rebellion of the companions in entering the earth-plane, it was necessary that there be a way of salvation. Here reincarnation becomes oddly Christianized in the Cayce readings, as Van Auken demonstrates in this reference to Christ:

> According to the secret teachings, the first soul to volunteer to go through every trial, overcome every temptation, dispel every illusion, conquer every challenge and reach perfection was that soul we call Jesus of Nazareth.

The story, taken as a whole, is a clever mixture of truth and fiction, so many people believe the basic premise. They may think that centaurs and mermaids are a bit much, and the cosmic significance of Snow White may be lost on them, but the rest of it seems reasonable enough. As Ms. MacLaine's friend David said of UFO's, "Why not? I feel comfortable with it."

Over the centuries, reincarnation has had a strong appeal even without such fanciful presentations. Plato, for example, believed in the soul's immortality. And, as Ms. MacLaine repeatedly reminds us in *Out on a Limb*, the list of historical figures who believed in reincarnation reads like a *Who's Who* of philosophers, scientists, theologians, politicians, and poets. Without doubt reincarnation is a captivating idea. After all, the prospect of many lives is alluring to those who fear extinction at death, or who shrink at the thought of eternal judgment and the fires of hell. Reincarnation has a ready market with all those who want to explain the sometimes unexplainable. It provides a worldview for those who have rejected traditional or religious paradigms. And speculation about past lives can even be entertaining.

One must remember, of course, that sheer numbers of supporters—even if great thinkers are included among the ranks—is no proof of a belief's validity. For example, in the early Christian centuries virtually the entire world population believed the earth to be flat, even though the Bible referred to God sitting "enthroned above the *circle* of the earth."

REALITY VERSUS FANTASY

I was in my favorite writing spot in Davos, Switzerland, as I read Van Auken's imaginative story about life's illusory nature. When I finished his Cayce-inspired account of the world's beginnings, I paused, letting his ideas run through my mind as I gazed around me.

The mid-June afternoon in the Dischmatal, a valley which headed eastward from where I lived on the edge of Davos, was bright with sunshine, replacing the cloudy gloom of the day before. On that lazy afternoon the fields were awash with every color of flowers, which light-tan cows were munching. White Silvermantle and Silvercoats, yellow and purple Roosterfeet (Hahenfuss), lilac-tinted and yellow mountain dandelions, delicate blue Ehrenpreis—the flowers were everywhere.

The little Dischmal creek rippled hurriedly over the large rocks lining the bottom as it wound its way past the quaint Alpine chalets, their window boxes splashed with red geraniums. Mothers with rosy-cheeked children, along with older couples showing years of alpine winters on their faces, greeted me with the local pleasantry, "Gruezi."

The Alps, always the silent backdrop for life in Davos, were standing on tiptoes, trying to touch the magnificent blue skies with their snowy peaks. As the cool breeze wafted down from their slopes and brushed against my face, I felt at one with the mountains, at one with the flowers and creek and cows and children, at one with nature. I also felt at one with God, and praised him for the glorious feeling of being alive and in this place!

As I walked along the Dischmal, I reflected on what Van Auken and others were saying—that who I am and what I perceive my world to be is merely an illusion. As I reached down to pick some of the flowers in the meadow, I was not convinced that either I or they were an illusion. And when I thought about the oneness I kept reading about in reincarnationist literature—that we are all one with the cosmos—I was sure something was wrong. I *knew* what it meant to feel like you are "one with nature." I was feeling it at that very moment. I had no doubt that nature and I were created by the same Creator, that the beauty I saw around me was not the result of cosmic accident, but was planned for human enjoyment by an artistically sensitive Personality who shared his love for aesthetics with his highest creation. But I knew that this was not what the reincarnationists were talking about. They were saying that we are one with *God*—that we ourselves actually are gods (or at least gods in the making) and are co-creators of our universe!

As I looked up at the Alps which towered above me on every side, I knew that this simply wasn't true. I knew that I couldn't even climb to the top of some of those peaks, much less *make* them.

And as I looked at the flowers in my hand, I knew again that the writers were wrong. We can build computers that mimic the human mind, but we can't make a single blade of grass!

If I cannot be the creator of my universe while in my physical body, there is no reason to believe I could ever have been its creator. According to the reincarnationists, I am the same entity I have always been from the beginning of time.

On that glorious afternoon high in the Swiss Alps, I knew what was real for me. We are the masters of the earth, but not its Maker. We did not create our world; we can only destroy it. And, as jets from the Swiss Air Force screeched through the sky overhead, disturbing the calm of the peaceful valley below, I was reminded that we destroy our earth with frightening ease and regularity.

Is life an illusion? Have we evolved from dryads and mermaids? Is our spiritual guidance to be found in children's fairy tales? Is our existence merely a futile attempt, over many lifetimes, to "get it right?" Is *that* what we are going out on a limb to believe?

Ironically, in *Out on a Limb* Shirley MacLaine repeatedly reminds us of the need to base our beliefs on *proof*, not blind acceptance. In that spirit, there are many hard questions to be asked of reincarnation!

✦

DON'T BELIEVE WHAT DOESN'T WORK

If cause-and-effect is applied consistently, so that spiritual ignorance or unenlightened personal conduct requires the learning experience of numerous lifetimes of trial and suffering, how can a person who is initially less than perfect ever hope to have an *upward* evolution? Trials and suffering often leave a legacy of bitterness, resentment, guilt, and hostility— the very traits which one presumably is trying to overcome. Wouldn't it be like a pilot whose plane is in a dive, finding himself unable to pull out of the dive because his own weight has been thrown against the stick? In such a spiral of cause and effect, the spiritually rich will get spiritually richer, but the spiritually poor will get spiritually poorer. Isn't this karmic quicksand?

Another problem with Westernized reincarnation lurks in the idea that we choose our supposed various lives on earth. If that were true, what accounts for the clear lack of choice we have over *continued* living? Ms. MacLaine's higher-self theory aside, unless one decides to cut short his life by suicide, no one has a choice about when or how he will die. If it were really true that we chose when and under what circumstances we would be born, why are we so helpless concerning the time and circumstances of our death? And if our destiny is sealed by our karma, how can *we ourselves* choose our next life?

Still another problem is a lack of proof. What is there in human experience to indicate that anyone has come close to achieving karmic balance, enlightenment, or spiritual perfection? It is not enough to say that those who have achieved oneness are obviously no longer reinvading the earth-plane.

In all of recorded human history, who *ever* traveled on a radically higher spiritual plane?

In response to that question, reincarnationists sometimes point to Buddha, or Krishna, or even Jesus. But the Bible explicitly tells us that Jesus Christ *came* from a higher dimension and then traveled back to that higher dimension which we call heaven. Jesus Christ is God by nature and became flesh to dwell among men. Neither Buddha nor Krishna have been historically documented to have traveled to any other dimension, much less a higher one. And there is no reason to believe that anyone else has ever evolved to some dramatically higher spiritual dimension. It's a question of cosmic paleontology: What evidence is there of any missing links? What evidence of evolutionary soul progression?

Even the practical details involved in reincarnation cause one to wonder. For example, I keep wondering how the cosmic shell game is played. When each soul has only one physical body, and each body has only one spiritual soul, there is no room for confusion or error in matching them. By contrast, the practical logistics problem facing the reincarnationists is enormous. Just imagine the billions of souls which must play musical chairs with the available bodies!

No matter how good a theory sounds, it still has to work. And that continues to be reincarnation's greatest problem: There is simply no evidence that it works—or that it ever has, or that it ever could. Where is the demonstrative evidence? What exhibits can the reincarnationists offer as proof?

THE PROVABLE FACT OF RESURRECTION

Unlike theoretical, speculative reincarnation, biblical resurrection is a provable, historical fact. Hundreds of people were witnesses to the death, burial, and resurrection of Jesus of Nazareth. Jesus' resurrection is a fact of history, the same as the D-day landing on the beaches of Normandy, the victory of the colonies in the American Revolutionary War, the defeat of Napoleon at Waterloo, and the ancient triumphs of Alexander the Great. Christ's resurrection really happened, and was as dramatic then as it would be today if one of your relatives who had died were to walk into your house with a resurrected body three days after being lowered into a grave in a sealed casket.

If Jesus Christ had never been raised from the dead, his teachings, wonderful as they are, would likely have been buried along with him. It is in the power of his resurrection that Jesus Christ becomes our hope and assurance. He is God's proof to the world of the resurrection to come and of eternal life for those who submit their lives to his lordship.

Of that event the witnesses have testified: "We are witnesses of everything he did in the country of the Jews and in Jerusalem. They killed him by hanging him on a tree, but God raised him from the dead on the third day and caused him to be seen" (Acts 10:39,40). The resurrection of Jesus is the ultimate historical fact. No other event in history has had, or ever will have, such powerful spiritual significance. "In the past God overlooked [spiritual] ignorance, but now he commands all people everywhere to repent. For he has set a day when he will judge the world with justice by the man he has appointed. He has given proof of this to all men by raising him from the dead" (Acts 17:30,31).

If it is proof that Ms. MacLaine is seeking, Jesus' resurrection is the verified exhibit upon which God rests his case. Compared with the speculative theory of reincarnation, Jesus' resurrection is evidence that demands a verdict. And for those who are willing to submit their lives to the lordship of Christ, the implication of this great historical fact is of utmost personal importance. "By his power God raised the Lord from the dead, and he will raise us also" (1 Corinthians 6:14).

CHAPTER SIX

MEMORY OR MAKE-BELIEVE?

"With how much ease believe we what we wish!"

—JOHN DRYDEN
All for Love

THE REINCARNATIONISTS HAVE HEARD the following challenge to their belief enough times for their patience to have earned them mountains of good karma, but it must be asked again: Why is it that nobody remembers their supposed past lives? Of the several answers offered by different reincarnationists, none is adequate to deal with the issue reasonably and convincingly. Some tell us there is a "veil of forgetfulness" that separates one lifetime from another. That's convenient, but entirely theoretical and unverifiable.

Others don't see our inability to remember as a problem at all, in light of the fact that we can't remember what we had for dinner on Tuesday night three weeks ago, much less what we were wearing on a given day when we were two months old. Granted that there is much in our present lives which is inconsequential and therefore forgettable, many events in our lives are remembered for decades. For example, I *do* remember that I was walking out of a chorus rehearsal in college when I heard that President Kennedy was assassinated. And in my mind's eye I can still see the television set that I was watching when our astronauts landed on the moon. Family weddings and funerals are still crisp in my mind, as are my graduation exercises and the swearing-in ceremony for my admission to the bar. The *important* events in my life are clearly in focus.

When it comes to remembering past lives, we're not asking for the color of our baby clothes, but for matters of real importance—such as how many times we've lived before, who we were, and especially what our bad karma is, so that we can start working on it. Why wouldn't we remember those important facts? Presumably it is because we are a completely different personality in each life—which raises an even more important question.

If we *can't* remember our past lives, *what good does it do us in this life?* How are we going to work out our bad karma if we don't even know what it is? This issue was raised in a passage from *Spring Snow*, a novel by the celebrated Japanese author Yukio Mishima, whose life story was recently made into a movie.

> The conversation [between Kiyoaki and Honda] then turned into a discussion of reincarnation itself and whether or not it was credible as a doctrine.
>
> "If there is such a thing as reincarnation," Honda began, betraying a certain eagerness, "I'd be very much in favor of it if it were the kind in your story, with the man himself being aware of his previous existence. But if it's a case of a man's personality coming to an end and his self-awareness being lost so that there's absolutely no trace of them in his next life, and if a completely new personality and a totally different self-awareness come into being, well, in that case I think that

various reincarnations extending over a period of time are no more significantly linked to one another than the lives of all the individuals who happen to be alive at the same given moment."

Through the fictional characters of the story, Mishima goes to the very core of the problem with the idea of reincarnation as it relates to working out one's karma. In real life, Mishima personally believed that the ultimate challenge in life was death itself. With such a low view of our present existence, it is probably not surprising that Mishima's life ended by *seppuku* (ritual suicide) at the age of 45.

If we really benefit from past-life experiences even though we can't remember them, then why in each new life do we have to start off as children again and relearn everything? Child prodigies are often cited as examples that not everyone must relearn basic human skills. Their special gifts are said to be "accumulated talent" from previous lives. But you can count child prodigies on one hand compared to all the children who have found staying within the lines of a coloring book to be a frustrating challenge. And even child prodigies have to learn to tie their shoelaces!

⋏

IMAGINED MEMORIES

Reincarnationists agree that there is no remembrance of previous lives—at least without assistance. But psychic mediums, hypnotists, and clairvoyants make it their business to conjure our past lives for us. Never mind that they must somehow penetrate the seemingly impenetrable "veil of forgetfulness" which hides the past from the ordinary person. And pity the millions of people who, unlike Shirley MacLaine, have lived and died without ever having had the opportunity to consult with cosmic private detectives such as Kevin Ryerson or Edgar Cayce.

Shirley MacLaine's latest attempt to discover her past lives has led her to try psychic acupuncture. In *Dancing in the Light*, Shirley tells about her travels through her own consciousness in search of past lives while her friend Chris stuck fine gold and silver needles into Shirley's body. Ms. MacLaine says that the acupuncture frees blockages in her mind and lets her communicate with the past through a kind of cellular memory.

Ms. MacLaine believes that she has both seen and talked to her higher self, her eternal unlimited soul—the soul that is the real "her." She believes that her higher self is the repository of her memory from lifetime to lifetime, that it knows all of her previous lives and personal experiences and can therefore guide her in her quest for enlightenment.

But how can Ms. MacLaine ever be sure that when she talks to herself it isn't just her lower self saying that she has a higher self? When her higher self is telling her that it remembers previous life experiences, how can Ms. MacLaine be certain that it isn't still just her lower self telling her what she wants to hear?

And even if Ms. MacLaine's higher self *were* the totality of her soul memory, what good does that do her lower self, which is unaware of why it is being guided in a certain direction by higher self? Trying to instill cosmic memory in a person by inventing a separate higher self doesn't solve the problem. For example, if lower self knew that higher self were luring him into an airplane destined to crash, the odds are that lower self would tell higher self to take a cosmic leap.

Shirley MacLaine herself has proved that point. On the "Larry King Live" show, Ms. MacLaine told King that if there are turbulent conditions while she is on an airplane, she imagines a bubble of light around the plane. She visualizes the plane as perfectly balanced so that it will not come to any harm. Is she saying that her "visualized balance" would have kept the Russians from shooting down the Korean Airlines jet? Could her "bubble of light" have kept the space shuttle Challenger from exploding? But more importantly, would she not be attempting to thwart what might be a larger cosmic choice being made by her higher self? In imagining her bubble of protection, is not Ms. MacLaine's lower self saying to her higher self, "*You* may have the cosmic game plan, but *I'm* the one who is going to have to fall 35,000 feet!"

Besides, if higher self already knows enough to guide lower self to enlightenment, then what need is there for lower self to begin with? If higher self is "part of God" and "totally aware," as Ms. MacLaine says, then what need is there for memory? Why the charade of multiple incarnations to achieve self-awareness?

WHY THE SIMILARITIES?

What strikes you as you turn each page of Shirley MacLaine's detailed past lives in *Dancing in the Light* is how similar the supposed personalities and circumstances are to relationships which Ms. MacLaine has already analyzed in her present life. For example, while experiencing acupuncture, Ms. MacLaine sees herself in a prior life in which she lived with a herd of elephants, and then wonders if that had anything to do with why she has a fascination with elephants in this life. Why doesn't it occur to her that she may have fantasized a past life with elephants because she likes elephants in *this* life? Another supposed past life takes place in the desert, and Ms. MacLaine speculates that it must be the reason why she has always felt a mystical attraction to the desert. Of course, she never admits the possibility that her past life in the desert had been conjured in harmony with her present attraction to the desert.

The obvious question is, Which came first: past-life experiences or present-life experiences? Is Ms. MacLaine attracted to the desert in this lifetime because she had a memorable experience there in a prior lifetime, or is her childhood fascination with the desert what leads her mind to construct an adventure in that setting? She acknowledges that one of her favorite childhood books was *The Sands of Karakorum*, a desert adventure story. Is it possible that under the influence of acupuncture her childhood story took on a cosmic interpretation?

When Ms. MacLaine's consciousness saw herself in Russia, serving at the royal court, there was an uncanny parallel between that experience and what she had experienced in this life with Vassy, her volatile Russian lover. Ms. MacLaine interpreted her vision as confirmation of certain conclusions she had previously drawn about their relationship. However, is it not just as possible that her mind was only confirming what she wanted to hear?

Don't we often dream about situations which are weighing heavily on our minds? And don't the characters in our dreams often seem terribly real, even if they are in a historical setting other than the present? The mind easily produces B-rated movies of things we are already thinking about.

Ms. MacLaine admits the possibility that she might just be making up her past life scenarios, but suggests that imagination is simply a form of memory. I suggest that it is just the opposite: To those who are looking for it, "memory" is simply the result of imagination.

✦

THE BIASED FINDINGS

One of the ways people are supposedly made aware of their past lives is through hypnotic regression. Data accumulated from such regressions is touted as substantial proof of reincarnation. Foremost among those who advocate such proof of "life before life" is Helen Wambach, author of a book by that title plus another book titled *Reliving Past Lives*. Of the latter book Ms. MacLaine recalls, "This book, perhaps more than any other, left no doubt in my mind that we have indeed lived past lives." The attention that Wambach's books have garnered is curious in view of her highly questionable scientific method.

Her findings are based upon various sessions in which she hypnotized groups of subjects—as many as 50 or more people at a time—and led them on what she calls a "birth trip." As she would look out on the relaxed bodies on the floor before her, Wambach would ask a series of questions for her subjects to reflect on while in the hypnotic state. Following the session, each participant would fill out a questionnaire indicating what they "saw" in response to the questions:

> "I want you to go now to the time just before you were born into your current lifetime. Are you choosing to be born?"

"Have you chosen your sex for this coming lifetime? If you have, why have you chosen to focus as a man or as a woman in this lifetime?"

"Now, I want to direct your attention to your mother-to-be [then father-to-be]. Have you known her [him] in a past life? If you have...what was your relationship before?"

"Are you aware now, before you are born, of others that you will know in the coming lifetime? Have you known them in past lifetimes? Do you know what role they will play in your coming life? Will you know them as lovers, or mates? Will you know them as children or other relatives? Will you know them as friends?"

As is evident from this sample of questions, Wambach began her study with the assumption that her subjects had experienced previous lives, and her subjects, for the most part, shared that assumption with her. Many of her subjects had been to Werner Erhard's est training or had been through the birthing process in therapy-oriented psychology workshops. Many had been through the Silva Mind Control training and a large number were into yoga. These New-Age-movement groupies were hardly a cross-section of the American public. We do not know what results would have been obtained from large groups of subjects who did *not* believe in reincarnation.

The predisposition of the test group is revealed in one of the responses to the wrap-up questionnaire: "My twin wanted to come into life at this time and talked me into going along with her. She seemed to have more karma to work out than I did, or at least was more eager to go." It is difficult to believe that such a karmic response would have been spontaneously, or even hypnotically, given by a nonbeliever or a person who had never heard of karma.

Wambach makes no secret of her subjects' predispositions. "Most of them," she says, "clearly had ideas in advance about whom they had been related to in past lives." And their responses generally indicate that what they saw under hypnosis were self-fulfilling prophecies. In referring to the difficulty that many of the subjects had in "seeing" what had happened to them in the actual birth process, Wambach observes, "In a sense, it was the veterans of the consciousness movement who tended to get the answers on the birth trips." Should that be surprising? A little cramming before the exam always helps!

Any theory of life that is based even partly on such flawed research should at the very least be highly suspect, and should certainly not be accepted as the basis for our eternal destiny!

✦

THE FRAUDULENT EDGAR CAYCE

Ms. Wambach's conclusions are not based upon scientific method but upon her personal belief in reincarnation and karma. In this point she follows squarely in the tradition of the "father" of American-style reincarnation, Edgar Cayce, who, like Kevin Ryerson and other psychics, claimed to be able to tell us about our past lives even when we don't remember them. When people look for proof of reincarnation, they inevitably turn to Cayce.

Who was this undisputed high priest of past lives, Edgar Cayce, whom Ms. MacLaine holds in the highest esteem? There are several notable oddities about Edgar Cayce's work.

First, it is curious—even suspicious—that so many past lives in his thousands of life readings turned out to be related to *Cayce's own* supposed past lives. The convenience of those associations is altogether too self-serving, suggesting that his life readings were simply the product of his own fertile imagination and not the result of any neutral supernatural source.

There is also cause for reasonable doubt when so many of the readings revealed that Cayce's friends and associates were previously famous figures in history. For example, the "adored nephew" of Cayce's secretary supposedly had been both Alexander the Great and Thomas Jefferson. Few of those whose "past lives" were read were ever just ordinary folk. Cayce's proclivity for sensationalism is certainly suspect.

Crucial to evaluating the validity of Cayce's past-life readings for other people are the many readings which supposedly revealed information about Cayce's own past lives. There are too many to review all of them, but some of them cast an interesting spotlight on this "king of karma." One appearance, for example, was about a thousand years after Adam. Cayce incarnated as the Egyptian high priest Ra Ta. During this incarnation, Cayce was instrumental in building the Great Pyramid (along with Hermes, who will later be seen as an especially significant entity). One account of this period is that—

> The Egyptians, in their cultural advancement over Arart's more pastoral and simple tribesmen, had long enjoyed lighter-than-air travel in gas-laden balloons introduced to them by the Atlanteans in times past.... Ra Ta saw an opportunity to visit other areas of the world where the sons of men

were gathered. So he went to India, to the Gobi land, to Og, and to what is now Peru, as well as to Carpathis. . . .

If Cayce's "reading" about himself is true, history books will have to be rewritten. As for the existence of the legendary Atlantis, Cayce interpreter Gina Cerminara says, "If the Cayce readings are to be accepted, Atlantis did very definitely exist." Of course it also means that, if Atlantis did *not* exist, Cayce's readings are *not* to be accepted.

As a soldier of Troy, Cayce helped defend the main gate of the besieged citadel. When the city fell, he was so humiliated that he committed suicide—truly a low point in Cayce's karmic evolution. Perhaps that accounts for the mistake in dates which Cayce obviously made in the reading. His reading (and not a subsequent recording error) indicates that he lived as the Trojan soldier from 1158 to 1012 B.C., a period of 146 years.

Never are Cayce's readings more outrageously inventive than when they turn to the supposed incarnations of Jesus, before he was Jesus. According to Cayce, Jesus incarnated as the biblical Adam, somewhere around 12,000 B.C. The implication that Jesus, therefore, was the one who committed Adam's sin was not lost on Cayce:

> "Q-3 *When did the knowledge come to Jesus that He was to be the Savior of the world?*"
> "When He fell in Eden. (2067-7)"

Jesus, our Savior, says Cayce, committed the original bad karma!

Cayce's next information from the "Memory of Nature," as he referred to the so-called omniscient Akashic Records, is a clear blunder. Cayce's readings said that Jesus also incarnated as Enoch, the man who did not die, but was taken up by God into heaven. Cayce has a major problem here, or perhaps it's a historical miscue by the Akashic Records. Jesus supposedly incarnated as both Adam and Enoch—*both of whom were living at the same time*! Although Enoch was born many years after Adam, Adam was still alive at the time of Enoch's birth, making the two of them contemporaries.

It was also said that Jesus manifested as Hermes, the architect of the Great Pyramid, whose colleague was Ra Ta (Cayce), and as Zend (father of Zoroaster), whose own father was Uhjltd (Cayce again). It's interesting how that works out. Jesus, the only begotten Son of *Cayce*? Perhaps it was all this cosmic closeness which gave Cayce the insight to know something the rest of us were never told—that, when Jesus finally incarnated *as Jesus* and was condemned to death, he "joked on the way to Calvary, as He carried His own cross."

After a while one has to stop and ask if anyone can have any faith in Cayce's life readings. The readings about his own supposed prior lives are preposterous and error-filled. And if that is true of the readings for his *own* "entity," what faith can we have that there is any truth to be found in the readings of other entities?

✦

SHIRLEY'S PSYCHIC, KEVIN

In the process of investigating psychic mediums, I arranged for a "channeling session" with Ms. MacLaine's personal psychic, Kevin Ryerson. Kevin played a prominent role in *Out on a Limb* and is also featured in Shirley MacLaine's television special, adapted from the book. Without revealing my involvement in the writing of this book (a fact which one might guess a genuine psychic would seize upon right away), I tried to appear as anyone else might who was sincerely seeking to know one's past. What I observed was that Kevin is not to be compared with your local palmist or crystal ball mystic at a two-dollar-entry-fee psychic fair.

Kevin is bright, articulate, thoughtful, and, for all appearances, sincere. He is well-read and conversant on such subjects as world religions, psychology, science, history, and philosophy. Coming from a mixed Presbyterian and Baptist background, he describes himself comfortably as a "Christian reincarnationist." Of course I couldn't disagree more with him regarding reincarnation, and especially his belief that it is compatible with Christianity. Yet if there were anyone I would enjoy spending the afternoon with talking about such esoteric matters, it would be Kevin.

What disturbed me most about Kevin was the "channeling" he supposedly was doing. Trying to be as objective as possible under the circumstances, I was not convinced that any astral-plane entities were using Kevin as their "instrument." The two voices of "John" and "Tom McPherson" seemed to me to be mere affectations of Kevin's own voice. I have spent a lot of time in England and Ireland, but never have I heard an Irish accent like the supposed voice of the entity "Tom," who is supposed to be Irish. Nor did it appear to me that Kevin was ever in what could fairly be called a trance state.

Curiously, responses from the entities could be obtained only after repeated questions from them regarding details of the inquiry. Such questioning would hardly seem necessary if the entities were in fact in tune with "the Universal

Mind." And despite an otherwise superb performance, there were lapses—sometimes rather long pauses—while a past life was being described for the listener. The hesitant pauses were not unlike those which you might observe on the part of people who are taking time to make up their answers— not at all consistent with the confident assurance you would expect from allegedly omniscient entities! On one occasion, as a test of factual accuracy, I purposely misrepresented that my mother was no longer living. The response to the question which I had posed wrongly assumed the truth of that misrepresentation. Wouldn't the Akashic Records *know* whether or not my mother were still on the earth-plane?

What I learned from "Tom" about my own past lives was that I had been born around 200 B.C. in India, into an upper Brahmin caste. I was a scholar, from a family which dealt extensively in trade along the Ganges. Well-steeped in the Vedic traditions, I practiced the so-called raja Yoga. When I was 28, I converted to Buddhism and traveled to Nepal. Appalled at the state of superstition and ignorance in the various mystery schools there, I taught them concerning Buddha and shared the enlightenment of the Brahmin traditions. I left that incarnation at the age of 97 while in a deep state of meditation.

In another lifetime I lived in Egypt as the son of a merchant family who had a monopoly from the Pharaohs in supplying the temples with oils, incenses, herbs, and materials for scrolls. Of mixed blood—Aryan, Semitic, and Nubian—I acted as a diplomat to help keep unity between the upper and lower kingdoms of Egypt. I left physical form at the ripe old age of 83, whereupon my body was embalmed.

It's one thing to be told that I have lived interesting past lives, but—surprise of all surprises—Shirley MacLaine can now add *me* to her ever-growing list of past-life relationships! According to "Spirit," as the entities are called, Ms. MacLaine and I were associated together as collaborators in China during the eleventh century. Ms. MacLaine was a shadow puppeteer and I was a Taoist scholar. We joined together in an effort to communicate Taoism to the people, using my scholastic knowledge and Ms. MacLaine's skills of communication through puppeteering.

I must confess that my supposed past-life association with Ms. MacLaine was nudged along by my own suggestion. It arose out of a dream which I asked to be interpreted. In the dream, Ms. MacLaine and I were together in Malibu. When I told "Spirit" about it, I specifically asked whether a prior lifetime with Ms. MacLaine might be a possible interpretation. Sure enough, it was! But I have the feeling that I might have missed out on my cosmic rendezvous with Shirley MacLaine had I not hinted at the possibility!

For all his innocent charm and genuinely likable personality, Kevin has no more access to universal consciousness than you or I. His supposed spiritual sources of cosmic information are best characterized as speculative and imagined. Kevin's act is simply one of the best road shows in America. Consummate lecturer, teacher, and personal adviser though he may be, tragically he is misleading the gullible regarding the true source of spiritual insight and the correct explanation of our spiritual destiny.

We must not forget that there is no independent verification available to show that anyone has actually experienced the previous lives which psychics like Edgar Cayce and Kevin Ryerson have claimed. The lack of independent corroboration constantly stalks them. But the flip side of that evidentiary gap is what keeps so-called psychics in business. They can pretend to see all the past lives they wish, with no threat of contradiction.

Shirley MacLaine has tied herself to a philosophical and evidentiary support base that defies both reason and experience. Whether under hypnosis or acupuncture, or with the aid and comfort of psychic mediums, you don't necessarily have to be scientific to "prove" the existence of prior lives. If someone *wants* to believe that he or she has lived before, it is easy to imagine it!

CHAPTER SEVEN

THE CUT-AND-PASTE BIBLE

"The Bible has often been treated as if it were a wax nose which may be twisted at the whim of the interpreter."

—CLARENCE TUCKER CRAIG
The Beginnings of Christianity

NOT ONLY HAVE REINCARNATIONISTS REJECTED the biblical promise of resurrection for the false hope of repeated lives, but they have also rejected a reasonable and coherent understanding of the Bible in favor of whimsical uses of biblical passages to support their theories. Let me explain what I mean.

When I was young, my father came home one night to relate a bizarre experience. Over several weeks he had studied the Bible with a man in our town who had shown an interest in learning more about Christianity. With patience Dad had carefully gone over a variety of doctrinal beliefs and shown the man the biblical passages which gave rise to those beliefs.

One week before, the man had angrily denied that one of the doctrines Dad was explaining could be God's will. He had never seen that particular teaching in the Bible and wasn't about to believe it. Again, Dad referred to the passages which he felt supported the doctrine, and said that perhaps he would like to think more about those Scriptures before their next meeting.

Dad went back to visit the man, not sure of what his reception would be. The man was surprisingly friendly, but said that there was no need to discuss any further the same doctrine they had discussed the week before. Dad asked if the man now understood that the teaching was biblical, but the man said, "No, those passages aren't in my Bible." Curious, Dad asked if he meant that they were there, but that he simply had a different understanding of them. Again the man replied, "No, they're not in my Bible."

Perhaps the man just couldn't locate the right passage, Dad thought. Dad took the man's Bible to open it to the proper passage. What Dad saw, much to his amazement, was that the passage was in fact not there. The man had taken a pair of scissors and literally cut it out of his Bible!

BENDING THE FACTS

If anyone but my father had told me that story, I would never have believed it. But there's an analogy here: Western reincarnationists, including Shirley MacLaine's spiritual mentors, treat the Bible the same way. Consistently they either "delete" passages from the Bible or so liberally read their own teachings into them that the Bible becomes one giant cut-and-paste job.

It would certainly make more sense and be easier for Western reincarnationists to just ignore the Bible, or else include it (as the Hindus often do) as only one "inspired but faulty" aspect of God's revelation. But old traditions die hard, especially for Westerners brought up in the culture (if not the instruction) of the Bible. It is more comfortable to accept reincarnation if someone can convince us that the Bible teaches it.

Truth, however, is not so accommodating as to allow for a selective approach to the Scriptures. By definition truth is transcendent reality: It is consistent, reliable, and universally applicable. We don't tend to be very flexible about truth when, for example, someone testifies against us in court, or the government sends us an income tax refund check for less than we expected!

There can be truth about which none of us has a perfectly clear picture—like the six blind men from Hindustan who each described a different part of an elephant. Each, based upon his personal experience, acquired part of the truth, but none had the whole truth. Yet there *is* factual truth about an elephant. The truth is that an elephant is not a lion, or a bird, or a basketball; and the fact that we might have a unique personal conception about it or decide to call it something else won't change the truth about what it actually is.

There is also truth about intangible, spirit things—such as God, and previous existence, and afterlife, and present life. And that truth is knowable. It is found not only within our own subjective experiences in our Creator's world but also through the objectively knowable revelation of the Bible.

Spiritual truth is by nature coherent and consistent: It does not contradict itself. It cannot accommodate both a belief that says we live many times on the earth and a contradictory belief that says we live only once. Truth cannot encompass both a belief that we can "do our own thing" until we "get it right" and a belief that we must do the will of our Maker and trust his righteous judgment.

THE SOURCE OF ALL TRUTH

The Bible claims exclusivity—that there is only one way.

This claim is foreign to the Eastern religions and unpopular among Westerners, who are traditionally democratic, independent, and pluralistic. Many fanciful dreamers have tried to embellish truth. Dreamers have tantalized the human imagination with tales, legends, and wonderful stories of the spiritual world. And the search for alternatives to sometimes-painful truth leads many people to pledge allegiance to myths.

However, Christianity brings a clear vision in the midst of this spiritual confusion—not simply because of a superior theological system or theory, but because of the person of Jesus, the Son of God, whose truth we seek and who is the world's Savior. Other religions are founded upon men—mere men—who do not have the power that comes from also being God, or upon abstract ideas or theories which know nothing of human reality. Jesus Christ, though God, was man in the flesh. Jesus Christ, though man, was and is the living God of creation.

In his commentary on the biblical letter to the Hebrews, Christian author John MacArthur, Jr., puts his finger on the superiority of Christianity. In every other religion the object is for man to find a way to God, whether it be by "escaping, or climbing, or thinking, or working" our way to him. In Christianity, God has brought himself to man.

That is the difference between Christianity and every other religion in the world. That is why it is so foolish for people to say, "It doesn't make any difference what you believe or what religion you follow." It makes every difference. Every religion is but man's attempt to discover God. Christianity is God bursting into man's world and showing and telling man what He is like. . . . He did it in human

form, and the name of that human form is Jesus
Christ.

Jesus is not just one among many spiritual guides. Con-
trary to Shirley MacLaine's attempt to equate the two,
Buddha is not on the same spiritual plateau as Jesus Christ.
He is not even close, because he was not God, as was Jesus.
If you carefully consider Jesus' teaching, you hear him say:

Enter through the narrow gate. For wide is the
gate and broad is the road that leads to destruction,
and many enter through it. But small is the gate
and narrow the road that leads to life, and only a
few find it.

I am the way and the truth and the life. No one
comes to the Father except through me.

They all asked, "Are you then the Son of God?"
He replied, "You are right in saying I am."

You are from below; I am from above. You are of
this world; I am not of this world. I told you that
you would die in your sins; if you do not believe
that I am the one I claim to be, you will indeed die
in your sins.

Do not be afraid of those who kill the body but
cannot kill the soul. Rather, be afraid of the one
who can destroy both soul and body in hell.

These are not the words of a wimpy, platitude-speaking
religious teacher, as Jesus is commonly portrayed. These are
not words that you can take or leave with impunity. Either

he actually is who he claims to be—the Son of God and source of all truth—or else he is an egocentric, blasphemous madman. Former agnostic and Cambridge University professor C. S. Lewis said it well:

> I am trying here to prevent anyone saying the really foolish thing that people often say about Him: "I'm ready to accept Jesus as a great moral teacher, but I don't accept His claim to be God." That is the one thing we must not say. A man who was merely a man and said the sort of things Jesus said would not be a great moral teacher. He would either be a lunatic—on a level with the man who says he is a poached egg—or else he would be the Devil of Hell. You must make your choice. Either this man was, and is, the Son of God; or else a madman or something worse. You can shut Him up for a fool, you can spit at Him and kill Him as a demon; or you can fall at His feet and call Him Lord and God. But let us not come up with any patronising nonsense about His being a great human teacher. He has not left that open to us. He did not intend to.

It is no wonder that the reincarnationist must deal with Jesus. The show cannot go on until we have heard from Jesus on the subject. What did the Son of God, the source of spiritual truth, say about reincarnation? Let's look first at what reincarnationists often claim for and about him.

WHAT JESUS DID AND DIDN'T SAY

When Shirley MacLaine listened to Kevin, he told her,

"Christ taught that a person's behavior would determine future events—or karma, as the Hindus say. What one sows, so shall he reap." When Ms. MacLaine talked to John, from the Bodhi Tree bookstore, John said that Moses and Christ "didn't always use the words karma or reincarnation, but the meaning was the same." When she listened to her friend David, David told Ms. MacLaine that Jesus said that "we had to understand that the soul and spirit of man had everlasting life and the soul's quest was to rise higher and higher toward perfection until we were free." He continued, "That's what Christ was trying to tell us. Everything we do or say in our lives every day has a consequence, and where we find ourselves today is the result of what we've done before." David concluded, "I'm convinced that Christ was teaching the theory of reincarnation."

A review of the passages presented by the reincarnationists as proof that Jesus taught reincarnation will give some insight into the issue. On one occasion Jesus was approached secretly by Nicodemus, a member of the Jewish ruling council. The following conversation ensued:

"Rabbi, we know you are a teacher who has come from God. For no one could perform the miraculous signs you are doing if God were not with him." [Jesus replied,] "I tell you the truth, unless a man is born again, he cannot see the kingdom of God." "How can a man be born when he is old?" Nicodemus asked. "Surely he cannot enter a second time into his mother's womb to be born!" Jesus answered, "I tell you the truth, unless a man is born of water and the Spirit, he cannot enter the kingdom of God.... You should not be surprised at my saying, 'You must be born again'" (John 3:2-7).

Is Jesus really teaching reincarnation here? He actually mentions only *one* rebirth, not many! And it is obvious that he rejected Nicodemus' suggestion that the rebirth would be through the womb. In fact, Jesus states plainly that the rebirth would be one of *water* and *spirit*. Paul refers to this rebirth of water and spirit in his letter to the Roman Christians:

> Don't you know that all of us who were baptized into Christ Jesus were baptized into his death? We were therefore buried with him through baptism into death in order that, just as Christ was raised from the dead through the glory of the Father, we too may live a new life.

It was *spiritual* rebirth through faith and the *water* of baptism to which Jesus was referring! It is this which brings a person new life in Christ. It has nothing whatever to do with multiple earthly lives; spiritual regeneration is its focus. It is the beginning of a new relationship of trust and commitment. A person who for the first time has experienced commitment to Christ literally feels like a *new person*—in the same body. It is plain that in teaching the need for spiritual rebirth, Jesus was not teaching the concept of reincarnation.

On another occasion Jesus was questioned by some of his disciples about a man who was blind:

> As he went along, he saw a man blind from birth. His disciples asked him, "Rabbi, who sinned, this man or his parents, that he was born blind?" (John 9:1,2).

In Jesus' day the Jews did not believe in reincarnation, but many Jews believed that sin is inherited from one's parents, who inherited it from their parents, and so on. Because of a misinterpretation of the Old Testament's emphasis on perfection as a reflection of God's glory, they also often associated physical imperfections as signs of sin (inherited or otherwise).

Jesus' response to this speculation was, in effect, You are wrong about that. "Neither this man nor his parents sinned," said Jesus, "but this happened so that the work of God might be displayed in his life." Jesus immediately healed the man, demonstrating his deity and his divine authority over creation.

I am mystified that reincarnationists would even bring up this passage for consideration, much less offer it as proof. Far from teaching reincarnation, it demonstrates that Jesus *specifically renounced* the idea that a person's state in this life is dependent upon anything from either someone else's life or from another life which he himself may have had. Even if one were not familiar with the doctrinal beliefs held by the Jews of that day, Jesus' teaching is plain on its face. "Whose sin caused this man to be blind?" they asked. Jesus responded, in effect, "Blindness is not caused by anyone's sin. Your belief in a cause-and-effect relationship here is simply wrong."

The next two passages offered as proof that Jesus taught reincarnation would only have merit if they were meant to be taken with wooden literality. As God's inerrant Word, the Bible is a beautiful literary work which displays every legitimate literary device, including figures of speech. At the close of some highly laudatory remarks about John the Baptist, Jesus made this observation:

For all the Prophets and the Law prophesied until

John. And if you are willing to accept it, he is the Elijah who was to come (Matthew 11:13,14).

Elijah was once again the subject of conversation when three of Jesus' disciples returned with Jesus from the transfiguration. Jesus had taken the disciples up on a mountain, and suddenly they saw Jesus talking with Moses and Elijah. It was more than a vision. Peter was so overwhelmed by the experience that he wanted to put up honorary shelters for each of them. (Moses and Elijah were actually called from the spirit world, which both affirms life after death and contradicts the theory of reincarnation.) On their way down the mountain following this experience, the disciples asked Jesus about the prophecies that Elijah was to come before the Messiah.

Jesus replied, "To be sure, Elijah comes and will restore all things. But I tell you, Elijah has already come, and they did not recognize him, but have done to him everything they wished. In the same way the Son of Man is going to suffer at their hands." Then the disciples understood that he was talking to them about John the Baptist (Matthew 17:11-13).

Had the ancient prophet Elijah been reincarnated as John the Baptist? Certainly not. Since John's mission was like Elijah's, John was being referred to symbolically as "the Elijah" of prophecy. When John's coming birth was first announced to his father by an angel of the Lord, the angel said:

Your wife Elizabeth will bear you a son, and you

are to give him the name John.... And he will go on before the Lord, *in the spirit and power of Elijah*, to turn the hearts of the fathers to their children and the disobedient to the wisdom of the righteous—to make ready a people prepared for the Lord (Luke 1:13,17).

Jesus' reference to John as Elijah is a common figure of speech. When a great young player comes onto the baseball scene, sportscaster Vin Sculley may say, "He is another Willy Mays or a Hank Aaron." In the same way, John's ministry was *reminiscent* of Elijah's. The disciples at the transfiguration understood Jesus' reference as a figure of speech because they had just seen Elijah—not their contemporary, John.

God provided a clear response to the reincarnationists' conjecture. In a passage which I have not seen mentioned in any of the reincarnation literature, John himself denied that he was the Elijah "entity" reincarnated:

Now this was John's testimony when the Jews of Jerusalem sent priests and Levites to ask him who he was. He did not fail to confess, but confessed freely, "I am not the Christ." They asked him, "Then who are you? *Are you Elijah?*" He said, "*I am not*" (John 1:19-21).

There is simply no honest way to put words of reincarnation in Jesus' mouth. Far from teaching the idea of reincarnation, Jesus taught that he can enrich our lives both now and in the *one* heavenly life to come. The promises he made are not karmic. They are assurances in which we can confidently put our faith:

Ask and it will be given to you; seek and you will find; knock and the door will be opened to you.

If a man is thirsty, let him come to me and drink. Whoever believes in me, as the Scripture has said, streams of living water will flow from within him.

Come to me, all you who are weary and burdened, and I will give you rest. Take my yoke upon you and learn from me, for I am gentle and humble in heart, and you will find rest for your souls. For my yoke is easy and my burden is light.

I am the resurrection and the life. He who believes in me will live, even though he dies; and whoever lives and believes in me will never die.

WHAT ABOUT KARMA?

We have seen clearly that neither the Bible nor Jesus Christ teaches reincarnation. But what about karma, the foundation of reincarnation belief? Does the Bible support the idea of karma?

In Shirley MacLaine's *Out on a Limb* and in virtually every other current book on reincarnation, the following phrase is used in connection with Christ's supposed teaching of reincarnation: "As you sow, so shall you reap." Each writer explains that Jesus is referring to the law of karma—that what a person has sown in a prior life will come back to meet him in a future life. If Jesus himself said that a man reaps what he sows, then, according to the reincarnationists, that should be the best evidence for reincarnation. Of course if Jesus said that, and meant what the reincarnationists say it means, then the reincarnationists would be right. That *would* be the best possible authority for such a belief.

In the one life we are now living, we *do* often reap what we sow. We *do* see instances of cause and effect. Everyone knows, for example, that smoking can cause cancer and that excessive drinking can lead to alcoholism. Failure to study is an open invitation to bad grades, and failure to pay taxes will get you into deep trouble. Trade deficits result in higher national debt, and abuse of personal freedoms eventually leads to revolution. In the ordinary affairs of this life, we *do* usually reap what we sow.

With this observation Jesus wholeheartedly agreed. For instance, Jesus referred to the wise man whose house stood firm on its rock foundation when a flood came, while the foolish man, who had built his house on the sand, watched his house collapse. The point of the analogy was that, just as physical actions have physical consequences, so moral actions have moral consequences.

Furthermore, Jesus plainly taught that we are not only *responsible* for our actions but also *accountable* for our actions. He repeatedly warned us that how we live in this life will have irrevocable eternal consequences. From Jesus' teachings we learn that the day of judgment will be a day of serious harvesting.

But never did Jesus teach that we will live many times on this earth in many different bodies as payment for our actions. Never did he teach that what we sow in one life will determine what we reap in another life on this earth. Never did he teach that sowing and reaping has anything to do with some cosmic law of karma. In fact the most amazing aspect of the reincarnationists' use of Jesus' supposed statement regarding sowing and reaping is that they are not even quoting the right source. *Jesus never said, "You reap what you sow"!* It is not simply a difference about what Jesus may have *meant*, but about what he never even said.

In the context of explaining the blessings one receives when he contributes to the financial welfare of his spiritual teachers, it was the *apostle Paul* who said:

> Do not be deceived: God cannot be mocked. *A man reaps what he sows.* The one who sows to please his sinful nature, from that nature will reap destruction; the one who sows to please the Spirit, from the Spirit will reap eternal life. Let us not become weary in doing good, for at the proper time we will reap a harvest if we do not give up. Therefore, as we have opportunity, let us do good to all people, especially to those who belong to the family of believers (Galatians 6:7-10).

Not only does the passage have nothing to do with reincarnation or karma, but it was said by *Paul*, not Jesus. When Ms. MacLaine's spiritual mentors answered her questions about Jesus' teaching, they simply misled her.

Unfortunately, their misinformation didn't stop with confusing what Jesus and Paul had to say. Shirley's friend David, for example, made a more serious mistake when he said, "To know yourself is the deepest knowledge of all. Christ said it: 'Know thyself.' And then be true to it."

Christ never said that! Nor did Paul or any other Christian writer. Such me-generation selfism couldn't be more in opposition to Christian teaching. "Know thyself" is a well-known ancient Greek admonition inscribed upon the Delphic oracle and attributed variously to Pythagoras, Socrates, Plato, or others long before Jesus lived. And it appears that David's last comment is a paraphrase of Shakespeare's "To thine own self be true," from Hamlet.

How can we possibly put our trust in someone who claims access to divine knowledge and then can't even attribute famous quotes to their proper author? Judges instruct jurors, "A witness found to be intentionally false in part of his testimony is to be distrusted in other parts of his testimony." Among the reincarnationists there is at least a callous disregard of easily knowable facts and a lack of full disclosure.

TRUE SOWING AND REAPING

Despite their quoting profusely from the Bible, it is obvious that reincarnationists have not carefully studied, or perhaps even completely read, the Bible. Ironically, it was in a discussion regarding the afterlife that Jesus told the Sadducees, "You are in error because you do not know the Scriptures." I wonder if in all of the reading which she did Shirley MacLaine herself ever sat down and read the Bible from cover to cover—carefully and prayerfully. Apparently she read some parts of it that were recommended to her, including some passages which are highly figurative and easily misunderstood by subjective personal interpretation. But it does not appear that Ms. MacLaine has a general understanding of the Bible. Otherwise she would have undoubtedly noticed the textual mistakes presented to her.

Jesus did teach on the subject of sowing and reaping. On

one occasion he used the word "reaping" to say that in God's great providence one need not be anxious about cause-and-effect prosperity.

> Therefore I tell you, do not worry about your life, what you will eat or drink; or about your body, what you will wear. Is not life more important than food, and the body more important than clothes? Look at the birds of the air; they do not sow or reap or store away in barns, and yet your heavenly Father feeds them. Are you not much more valuable than they? Who of you by worrying can add a single hour to his life?

What Jesus taught about sowing and reaping was not karmic cause and effect. In Christ we reap the spiritual benefits of what others before us have sown on our behalf. In Christ we reap much more in spiritual blessings than we ourselves have sown. And if we have submitted our lives to the lordship of Jesus Christ, we are promised that God will provide for us even when our sowing has been inadequate. According to Jesus, we don't karmically get what we deserve. We get *far better* than what we deserve!

CHAPTER EIGHT
JESUS—YOGI OR SAVIOR?

"It were better to have no opinion of God at all than such a one as is unworthy of him; for the one is only unbelief—the other is contempt."

—PLUTARCH

THE CASE BEING PRESENTED for New-Age, Westernized, Christianized reincarnation is a lot like a murder case I once tried. Counsel for the defense presented the jury with two inconsistent theories: Either the defendant accidentally shot his girlfriend, or else he acted in self-defense—take your pick! Which theory the jury happened to like hardly mattered as long as the attorneys got a Not Guilty verdict, even if it meant that they had to employ two theories which argued against each other.

In the case being presented to us by reincarnationists, there is also a lot of alternative pleading going on that is neither logically consistent nor even honest. We are first told that Jesus Christ himself taught reincarnation. When the patent weakness of that argument is brought out on close cross-examination, we are told that there is a second theory, which turns out to be inconsistent with the first theory.

In this second theory we are told that it really doesn't make any difference what Jesus said because he wasn't really the Son of God after all. He was a *good* man, and perhaps one of the most moral persons ever to have lived. But certainly he was not God revealed in the flesh. And by no means was he the absolute, exclusive source of spiritual truth. He was more like the Jesus that Shirley MacLaine had grown up believing:

> Jesus Christ seemed like a smart, wise, and certainly a good man, but I viewed what I learned about him in the Bible as philosophical, mythological, and somehow detached. What he preached and did didn't really touch me, so I didn't believe or disbelieve. He just happened...like all of us...and he did some good things a long time ago. I took his being the Son of God with a grain of salt, and, in fact, by the time I was in my late teens, had decided for myself that God and religion were definitely mythological and if people needed to believe in it that was okay with me, but I couldn't.

Ms. MacLaine has well summarized what a large segment of our society has come to believe about Jesus. In her book, *Many Mansions*, Gina Cerminara, the chronicler of Edgar Cayce's readings, is quite comfortable putting other people on a spiritual par with Jesus:

> The Christ-consciousness is not, however, an exclusively Christian attribute. Christ, it must be remembered, is not the name of the man Jesus, but a term whose literal meaning is "the anointed one," and whose mystic or rather psychological meaning is that of the liberated or spiritual consciousness. Krishna and Buddha were, we may believe, equally the possessors of Christ-consciousness. . . .

Even *we*, she goes on to say, may achieve Christ-conscious-
ness—not meaning simply that we can "put on the mind
of Christ," as the Bible says, but that we can literally become
our own Savior! Invariably, Shirley MacLaine also speaks of
Christ and Buddha in the same breath, as if they were
spiritual equals—as if Buddha was also born of a virgin, as
if Buddha could also command stormy waves to be still or
bring people back from the dead, and as if Buddha was also
resurrected three days after his own death!

THE MYSTIC MYTHS

It is not enough that the case against Jesus attempts to present him as something less than God. Another facet of this
second theory presented in the reincarnationists' trial of
Jesus is the allegation that Jesus was the product of Eastern
mysticism. Remember the 18 years of Jesus' life for which
there is no explicit record of events in the Bible—the years
between the time Jesus was 12 years old and the time he
began his public ministry at the age of 30? Some people
think they know what Jesus was doing during that time.
They claim that Jesus wasn't the carpenter we have read
about in the Bible. Depending on who you talk to, Jesus
either was educated by the Essenes or became a guru, an
avatar, or a Yogi—or all of the above!

That's what Kevin told Ms. MacLaine, and David echoed
those thoughts:

> . . .a lot of people think that those eighteen miss-
> ing years were spent traveling in and around India
> and Tibet and Persia and the Near East. There are
> all kinds of legends and stories about a man who

sounds just like Christ. . . . They say he became an adept yogi and mastered complete control over his body and the physical world around him. He evidently went around doing all those miracles that were recorded later in the Bible and tried to teach people that they could do the same things too if they got more in touch with their spiritual selves and their own potential power.

Ms. MacLaine was already familiar with the theory, from having met Janet and Richard Bock at the Ashram. The Bocks have spent considerable time and effort chasing down the various legends that say Jesus traveled to India and Tibet.

In Janet Bocks' *The Jesus Mystery*, it is clear that many Eastern mystics want to lay claim to Jesus. Swami Prajnananda told the Bocks that "Christ was an Indian Yogi." In fact, the Swami said that Christ "realized God as not only Christian, but Hindu, Jain, Buddhist and the God of all faiths." His Holiness Muni Shshil Kumarji, a Jain monk and leader, told the Bocks that Jesus had also spent time with *his* people!

As for an explanation of Jesus' extraordinary power over the forces of nature, it was his experience in becoming a Yogi, says Bock, that permitted Jesus the ability to perform his miracles.

But is there any evidence that a mere Yogi could calm the waves of a storm-tossed sea, or feed 5000 people with a few loaves of bread and a couple of fish? Would any present-day Yogi even attempt such feats?

THE EIGHTEEN YEARS

As for the 18 years themselves, if Jesus had been in India

all of those years, wouldn't there be some mention of it by Jesus' family? His brothers, who did not accept Jesus as the Christ until after his crucifixion and resurrection, taunted him about his ministry, but never once did they attribute what he was doing to trips to Tibet or India.

The same is true of Jesus' neighbors and the people of Nazareth where Jesus grew up. Although many of them rejected Jesus as the Messiah, they never related that rejection to Jesus being a Yogi or avatar. No one said, "Well, what can you expect from someone who's been hanging around the ashrams of India?"

When Jesus was publicly charged with blasphemy by the Jewish leaders, it was *not* for being into Eastern mysticism, but for claiming to be the promised Messiah. In fact, one of the arguments offered in support of the charge of false impersonation was that Jesus had been among the local townspeople all this time! "But we know where this man is from," they insisted, "when the Christ comes, no one will know where he is from."

"Isn't this the carpenter?" asked the local townspeople. It's as if they were saying, "We *know* Jesus couldn't be the Messiah, because he's lived just down the street from us all these years, working as a carpenter. Now all of a sudden he is claiming to be the Messiah. Who would have believed it possible!"

How did the mystic legends about Jesus get started? It is highly likely that word of the holy man from Palestine was indeed carried by merchant trains to distant lands, including India. In fact, it would be quite surprising if news about Jesus had *not* spread that far. Once the story of Jesus started making the circuit, particularly within different religious groups, it undoubtedly was modified in order to be more consistent with locally accepted beliefs. The best example of how this phenomenon works is the way in which the

Eastern theory of reincarnation has been Christianized for Western ears.

There is this much to be said: Anyone wanting to dismiss Jesus as a merely mythological figure will have to think twice. Even the *counterfeit* evidence about Jesus gives added support to the historical fact of his life and ministry!

CHOICE WITHOUT COMPROMISE

As the modern-day trial of Jesus is presented to us, the tactics of the reincarnationists are clear. They have tried first of all to use Jesus in their own self-defense, hoping that what he taught could be interpreted in such a way as to save their threatened theory. But if we see through that defense, they ask us to see what a mistake has been made about Jesus: He wasn't really the Son of God, as he claimed to be, but only a very good man and a master teacher—perhaps even a Yogi, avatar, or co-equal with Buddha.

The essence of the case is whether we believe the Bible's claims about Jesus. In writing to the Christians at Colosse, the apostle Paul placed the issue clearly in focus:

> He is the image of the invisible God, the first-born over all creation. For by him all things were created: things in heaven and on earth, visible and invisible, whether thrones or powers or rulers or authorities; all things were created by him and for him. He is before all things, and in him all things hold together.
>
> And he is the head of the body, the church; he is the beginning and the firstborn from among the

dead, so that in everything he might have the supremacy.

For God was pleased to have all his fullness dwell in him, and through him to reconcile to himself all things, whether things on earth or things in heaven, by making peace through his blood, shed on the cross.

Unlike a jury in a murder case, we are not permitted the luxury of a compromise verdict. The Bible's affirmations about Jesus require that we either accept him as our one and only Lord and Savior, or else reject him altogether.

Was Jesus merely a meditating Yogi, a dancing Krishna, or a smiling guru? Or was Jesus the Lord of all Creation, the source of all truth, the Savior of the world, and the very Son of God, before whom at the day of judgment every knee will bow—Buddha's, Krishna's, Janet Bock's, Shirley MacLaine's, yours, and mine!

CHAPTER NINE

A REINCARNATION WATERGATE?

"In the hands of unbelief, half-truths are made to do the work of whole falsehoods."

—ENOCH FITCH BURR

WE HAVE EXAMINED reincarnationists' misuse and misinterpretation of the Bible in their attempt to gain support for their views from the Bible. But there is another way that reincarnationists often argue that their views are compatible with Christianity. Instead of starting with the assumption that the Bible is God's infallible Word, reincarnationists often argue that the Bible is incomplete in its revelation, that important truths have been lost or deliberately omitted, or even that the Bible was drawn from Eastern reincarnationist literature.

For example, after explaining to Ms. MacLaine the significance of the Akashic Records, "John" (a composite character representing owner and staff of Ms. MacLaine's favorite metaphysical bookstore) had raised a question about the Bible's inspiration, implying that the Akashic Records had in some way been involved in the revelation given to the biblical writers:

For example, how do you think Moses wrote of

the creation of the world if he hadn't been plugged in psychically? And the same with Christ. I mean, those guys were highly developed spiritual people who felt their mission in life was to impart their knowledge.

John went on to concede that Jesus never actually used the word "reincarnation," but that the meaning was the same. After all, he did talk about laws of morality and an eternal soul!

> "Well," [Shirley asked,] "what did they say about *not* remembering your former lives?" [John replied:] "They talk about a kind of 'veil of forget-fulness' that exists in the conscious mind so that we aren't continually traumatized by what might have occurred before. They all say that the *present* lifetime is the important one, only sparked now and then by those deja-vu feelings that you have experienced something before or know someone that you know you've never consciously met before in this lifetime."

John's allusion to the Bible referring to anything like deja vu or a "veil of forgetfulness" is made up out of thin air. One can search the Bible from cover to cover and never find either of those concepts mentioned—not even once, even vaguely.

CALLING THE JAILER

Such artificial machinations remind me of a familiar

courthouse story of a defense counsel's desperate ploy in a case where there was absolutely no evidence in favor of his client. In the closing argument, he asked the jury why the prosecution had not brought in the jailer to testify. "Why hasn't *the jailer* been brought in to testify in this case?" he demanded loudly. "What do they have to hide?"

Of course, the jailer had no information whatever about the case, one way or the other, but the jury didn't know that. And the defense counsel was gambling that no one on the jury would realize that he himself could have subpoenaed the jailer. By the time the defense counsel had finished his grandstand play about the jailer, the jury was certain that a piece of important evidence was deliberately being withheld from them.

What is the prosecutor to do in a situation like that? Naturally, he will get up in his closing argument and deny it: "The jailer doesn't know anything about this case." *Sure*, the now-skeptical jurors think!

It's an effective ploy. Shout something loudly enough and a lot of people will believe you, even if what you are saying has no factual basis whatsoever. Unfortunately, Ms. MacLaine was the recipient of truckloads of such contrived information. Both Kevin and David used the ploy, whether intentionally or otherwise. Nowhere is this more evident than in their references to alleged secret deletions of significant teachings from the Bible:

> There's a phrase in the Bible [Kevin says] which states that one should never countenance spiritual entities other than God. Most Christians go by that. But then the Bible says nothing about reincarnation either. . .and it's quite well known that the Council

of Nicea voted to strike the teaching of reincarnation from the Bible.

Kevin presumably is saying that the Bible at one time contained reincarnation teaching, but that the early fourth-century church ordered those portions of the Scriptures ripped out, cut out, burned, or otherwise destroyed. Fortunately, there are volumes and volumes of church history records which cover minutely the contents, actions, and resolutions of the Council of Nicea and the history of the early church. No responsible historian, taking into account all of the records available to us, will agree with Kevin that reincarnation had anything to do with either the council, the original content of the Bible, or the soundness of church doctrine.

Even the logistics of such a conspiracy strain one's credulity. How could the church have gotten access to all the copies of Scripture which had come into existence over the prior two centuries? How could we account for the manuscripts we possess which were composed before then, and which match the text we have today, but which have no mention of reincarnation? How could we account for the fact that the early church lectionaries (collections of Bible readings to be used in worship services), from which we can recreate the text of virtually the entire New Testament, universally ignored what Kevin assumes was a central biblical teaching? And could we reconcile the two mutually-exclusive teachings of resurrection versus reincarnation in one unified Bible? How could the editing process avoid causing noticeable gaps in the biblical records? Why was no record of the deleted passages made from the memory of any pro-reincarnationists who might have been living at the time, since this would have been a deletion of the greatest historical and spiritual magnitude to them?

When Ms. MacLaine pressed Kevin as to how he knew about this alleged Nicean action, Kevin responded, "Well, most serious metaphysical students of the Bible know that. The Council of Nicea altered many of the interpretations of the Bible."

The question actually before the council involved the nature of the deity of Christ. It is a matter which should be considered more carefully by reincarnationists, since they universally deny Christ's unique divinity. But the issue itself was not reincaration. The issue was whether Christ, the Son, had eternally coexisted with God the Father, or whether he was the first of God's *spiritual* creation before the creation of the world. Simply stated, was Christ fully equal with God? That question was important in resolving the issue of the Trinity—i.e., Father, Son, and Holy Spirit.

A second, lesser issue before the council was whether the historical Jesus was God in a human body, or whether Jesus was merely given a special measure of divinity. Ironically, the issue arose because some people had begun to claim that Jesus was a good moral teacher but not really Deity—the same message we have been hearing from those in the New Age movement!

It is easy to see what the controversy was all about by simply reading what the Council decided, which was formulated in a widely published creed that has been recited regularly from then until now, part of which reads:

> We believe in one Lord, Jesus Christ, the only Son of God, eternally begotten of the Father. . . . God from God, Light from Light, true God from true God, begotten, not made, one in Being with the Father.

As is too often the case among the proponents of reincarnation, Kevin lost sight of the difference between truth and fiction. And I am curious about that. Is playing fast and loose with historical facts what we can expect from mediums who are supposedly in touch with the omniscient Akashic Records? Are mediums given special permission to operate in the twilight zone of truth where innuendos so easily entice the gullible?

DAVID AND THE COUNCIL

Naturally, David also told Ms. MacLaine about the church's alleged "Reincarnation Watergate":

> The theory of reincarnation is recorded in the Bible. But the proper interpretations were struck from it during an Ecumenical Council meeting of the Catholic Church in Constantinople sometime around 553 A.D., called the Council of Nicea. The Council members voted to strike those teachings from the Bible in order to solidify Church control. Anyway, that's what I believe Christ was really doing and when the Church destroyed those teachings, it screwed up mankind from then on.

Tragically, David reveals a blatant disregard for the truth. The Council of Nicea was convened by Constantine in A.D. 325, not 553. The council which met in A.D. 553 was the Fifth Ecumenical Council, known as Constantinople II. At that later council several issues were under discussion, but none dealt with reincarnation. Interestingly, one of the issues which *was* discussed gave rise to what Ms. MacLaine later read from *The Catholic Encyclopedia*, which stated that "anyone asserting the belief in the preexistence of souls" would be anathema (officially denounced).

This was the council's reponse to a teaching which had persisted from the third century, at which time a theologian named Origen speculated that the soul was *preexistent*— not that it had experienced previous incarnations, but only that it had existed prior to a person's birth.

In his earlier works, Origen had taught that humans had once been *angelic* creatures, and, in karmic fashion, were affected in this life, depending on whether they had been bad or good in their *angelic* existence. However, just as Origen rejected *previous* incarnations, he also rejected the idea that there would be *future* incarnations.

In commenting on the previously discussed theory that John the Baptist was a reincarnation of the prophet Elijah, Origen wrote:

> In this place, it does not appear to me that by Elijah the soul is spoken of, lest I fall into the dogma of transmigration [reincarnation], which is foreign to the Church of God and not handed down by the Apostles, nor anywhere set forth in the Scriptures. For observe, [Matthew] did not say, in the "soul" of Elijah, in which case the doctrine of transmigration might have some ground, but "in the spirit and power of Elijah."

It is noteworthy that, writing at least 70 years before the Council of Nicea and some 300 years before Constantinople II, Origin himself indicated that there was no teaching of reincarnation in either the Bible itself, the apostles' teaching, or the church.

As for the anathema against the teaching of preexistence, the church condemned it not because it threatened church doctrine but because such a notion is not taught in the Bible. More importantly, never once in the first millennium did the church officially even *consider* the idea of reincarnation, much less deliberately alter the Bible to eliminate it.

If, in fact, such an effort had been undertaken by the church, why is it that there are still so many alleged proof texts for reincarnation in the Bible? For example, if Paul's statement that "as a man sows, so shall he reap" is really karmic teaching, then why wasn't *that* passage deleted? Why wasn't Jesus' statement about Elijah and John the Baptist eliminated? The same goes for the dozen or so other favorite passages which have been reinterpreted by the reincarnationists.

There is also abundant evidence that the church never *added* passages which directly contradict the notion of reincarnation. Original to the Bible is the passage *"Man is destined to die once, and after that to face judgment"* (Hebrews 9:27). Paul's letters to the Thessalonian and Corinthian Christians are filled with *resurrection* teaching, which is completely incompatible with the teaching of reincarnation.

✦

ALL THE PIECES FIT

It all gets to be ridiculous after a while. And an important fact is lost sight of along the way: When you read the Bible from cover to cover, especially in chronological order, what you see is an incredible unity and harmony in all the diverse writings of Scripture which we call the Bible. As we have received those collected Scriptures, *all the pieces fit*. Even John from the Bodhi Tree admitted that much: "Most all of their writings jibe too," he told Ms. MacLaine.

Biblical history fits with secular history; great themes from the law and the prophets fit with the great themes of the Messiah and the writings of the apostles; prophecies during the more than 2000 years before Christ fit, *in detail*, with the life of Jesus. If the Bible were the product of the alterations, mistranslations, and private interpretations which are alleged, the pieces simply wouldn't fit as they do.

Looking at the Bible as a whole, you find Abraham and the patriarchs "going to their fathers" or "being gathered to their people" when they die. You hear David saying of his son who has died, "I will go to him, but he will not return to me."

In one of their psalms, the sons of Korah ask rhetorically, "Do those who are dead rise up and praise you?" In his wise sayings, Agur asks, "Who has gone up to heaven and come down?... Tell me if you know!" When contemplating his death, King Hezekiah of Judah laments, "I will not again see the Lord...in the land of the living; no longer will I look on mankind, or be with those who now dwell in this world."

The single most instructive writing in all the Bible on the subject of life and afterlife is the book of Ecclesiastes, written by King Solomon, who was renowned for his God-given gift of wisdom. Solomon asks the pivotal question, Who can tell us what will happen after a person is gone? Man can no more prevent his own death than can an animal. Our bodies—whether animal or human—deteriorate, die, and decay.

We don't choose when we go, any more than we choose when we come. Therefore we must find life's meaning in the time we have on the earth. Afterward it will be too late.

Will the dead return to this earth? No, says Solomon: *"Never again will they have a part in anything that happens under the sun."* Therefore he counsels, "Whatever your hand finds to do, do it with all your might, for in the grave, where you are going, there is neither working nor planning nor knowledge nor wisdom." According to Solomon, any notion like reincarnation is a mere fantasy.

OUR PURPOSE IN LIVING

What is our purpose in living? Not any of the usual things we chase around doing. I think Ms. MacLaine would like what Solomon says here. He says we are only fooling ourselves in thinking that achievement, pleasure, materialism, politics, popularity, and power are what life is all about. After all, Solomon agrees, you can't take any of those things with you when you go!

So then what is life all about? It is about things that are eternal. God, says Solomon, "has set eternity in the hearts of men." That is how we are different from animals. We each have a soul that lives beyond death. And we will one day be judged as to how well we have prepared our soul for its afterlife.

Therefore, Solomon concludes, "Remember your Creator. . .before. . .the dust returns to the ground it came from, and the spirit returns to God who gave it."

It wasn't some ancient church council that changed what the Bible had to say about life and afterlife. It is the reincarnationists themselves who deceive (knowingly or unknowingly) gullible people into believing that the Bible we have today is not what was originally given and preserved by God.

If the jailer *were* to take the witness stand, he would be testifying honestly when he tells us that he knows nothing about any alleged reincarnation Watergate. But he could also tell us that there are people who find themselves in his custody for perpetrating a fraud on the public. Perhaps the reincarnationists should give that some thought. There is a Judge who is taking a keen interest in what they are going around telling people. "For God," says Solomon, "will bring every deed into judgment, including every hidden thing, whether it is good or evil."

CHAPTER TEN

UNCARING KARMA

"I am no more of a Christian than Pilate was, or you are, gentle hearer; and yet, like Pilate, I greatly prefer Jesus of Nazareth to Amos or Caiaphas; and I am ready to admit that I see no way out of the world's misery but the way which would have been found by his will."

—GEORGE BERNARD SHAW

NOT ONLY DO REINCARNATIONISTS falsely assert that the Bible has been altered to omit reincarnationist teachings, but they also wrongly assert that the doctrine of karma is better and more fair to mankind than Christian beliefs. Clinging to the false security of cosmic retribution, reincarnationists risk drowning spiritually for refusing to reach out to the lifeline of God's dynamic love and grace toward imperfect mankind.

Impersonal law cannot dispense grace since grace is undeserved favor that requires intelligence and compassion accompanied by a dynamic relationship between the dispenser of justice and the accused. Let me illustrate what I mean by something that happened to me as a District Attorney.

I received a phone call from an attorney who gave me the details of his client's predicament. It seems that the client was caught between two computers and the State Police. When the computer at his insurance company didn't kick out the right form, showing proof of coverage, the computer at the Department of Motor Vehicles kicked out a notice of license suspension and notified the State Police. The State Police were then required to arrest the man if they saw him driving on the highways, which he had to do if he wanted to keep his job.

The man was arrested twice for "driving while suspended," each time explaining how he had done everything he could do to straighten out the paperwork. Dealing with computers can be maddening enough for anybody, but to add to the problem in this case, the client was not a particularly bright individual. Even the officer who had issued the most recent ticket confirmed that it was a senseless situation.

No problem, I told the attorney. I would just call the Justice of the Peace and dismiss the charge in the interest of justice. Dismissing a charge is routine. Most judges have quite enough cases to keep them busy, and part of a District Attorney's job is to exercise discretion in hard cases. But, to my surprise, the Justice of the Peace—an elderly man who once had my job as D.A. but was now semiretired—refused to grant the dismissal. No explanation was given. "Well," I said, "I just won't show up for trial." "Then I'll try the case without you," the judge responded curtly.

Faced with that prospect, I informed both the defendant's attorney and the arresting officer that we would need to go ahead with the trial. At the appointed time, we met in the little courtroom, along with the six busy farmers who had been called out of their potato fields for the day to serve as jurors.

It didn't take long to put the officer on the stand and glean the basic facts proving the prima facie case. I rested the state's case and listened as the defendant told his story, with the aid of his attorney's questioning. Once again, his story sounded both believable and reasonable.

When it came time for arguments to the jury, I felt apologetic—and told them so—for having to waste their time. "I'm in a most unusual situation," I told them. "Without doubt, there is a violation of the law here, technically speaking, but you've heard the defendant's story, and it makes a lot of sense to me. It seems to me he's done all he could do to comply with the law. Therefore, I am asking you to return a verdict of Not Guilty."

Red-faced with anger, the judge slammed his gavel down and threatened to hold me in contempt of court. "Mr. District Attorney," he almost screamed, "your duty is to prosecute!" "I'm sorry, Your Honor," I replied, "but I am sworn to do justice." At that, and with surprised looks from the jurors, the judge mumbled angrily to himself and settled back in his chair.

The defendant's attorney got up slowly and sort of shook his head. "What can I tell you, gentlemen? In this case we wholeheartedly agree with the prosecution!" Within five minutes we *both* got a Not Guilty verdict from six very upset potato farmers.

THE DIFFERENCE BETWEEN KARMA AND GOD

Left to the law alone, and even to an insensitive judge, the defendant would have been found guilty. If cause and effect had been allowed to rule the court, karma would have convicted the poor man. That's the difference between karma and God. God has sworn to do justice, and when we have committed our lives to Christ, he will not find us guilty—

even if we actually are sinners. The core of biblical salvation teaching is that, because no man is perfect and therefore is unable to perfectly fulfill the law of God, salvation can only come through our own personal choice of Christ as our sacrifice for sin and as our advocate (defense attorney) with the Father. This doesn't mean that we can plead ignorance of God's laws, or act irresponsibly in refusing to obey them. But it does mean that, when we have done all we can do to obey his will and still fall short, we can choose Christ as our Savior.

By contrast, there is no one to plead our cause in the courts of karma. In fact, it's almost an exaggeration to say that karma has any courts at all. Karma is more like a cosmic governmental administrative agency, open to serve the public only during strictly limited hours.

The really frightening thing about karma is not so much that it is neither empathetic nor merciful—which it is not— but that there is not even any evidence that it is intelligent. When we consider a God intelligent enough to create the universe, then we can at least assume his ability to deal with *us* intelligently! But with karma we have no such assurance. All we have to go on is a theoretical principle which cannot adapt itself to any real-life situation.

It is not difficult to see that the law of cause and effect has significant limitations in the area of human actions and relations. In the unexpected realities of life, the race is not necessarily won by the fastest runner, nor war by the strongest army. Just ask Olympic runner Mary Decker Slaney or the veterans of Vietnam. Nor does abundance always come to those who are wise, or wealth to the brightest among us.

God is aware of life's inequities. But what assurance can we have that the impersonal law of karma can intelligently relate to our human situation in the same way? Dealing with the law of karma is like having to deal with the person on the lowest level of an organization. We have all frequently heard the excuse "I'm only doing what I'm told." Is *that* who we want to deal with, or the *person in charge* who can make the exceptions when the case warrants it?

It's not only karma's judgment that I worry about. Have you heard about its sentencing record? I have seen some tragic sentences handed out, but nothing to compare with what we are told happens when karma sits on the bench. For example, according to the Cayce readings, as presented by Gina Cerminara, any birth abnormality "is probably of karmic origin."

Birth defects happen to the child, reincarnationists preach, because of his or her past-life transgressions. And in having such a child the parents are usually working out some past-life karma as well. Cerminara continues: "Again and again, in [Cayce's] readings taken on children suffering with mongolian idiocy, deafness, water on the brain, and many other tragic afflictions, one finds the phrase: 'This is karma, for both the parent and the child.' "

The most offensive aspect of all of this is that Cerminara says regarding those whose children are born with birth defects: "To such parents the reincarnation principle can be a source of reassurance and courage." Even Shirley MacLaine finds karma to be a comforting explanation for such things as infant deaths.

Would you want to "comfort" your friends on the birth of their handicapped baby by walking into the hospital room where their deformed baby lies, and announcing with confidence that there is nothing to worry about—that all of them deserve what happened, and that this is just karma's way of helping both the child and the parents evolve to a higher level of enlightenment?

ᛉ

NO FIERCE GOD IN THE SKY

John Van Auken is quite proud of the fact that karma "is not some fierce god in the sky keeping track of everything people do so it can zap them when they least expect it." I'm happy to say that this is not what the God of the Bible is either, though I can't say as much for karma, which zaps children with deformities because of past-life misdeeds! But Van Auken says we must see the benefits behind such zapping. "The law is actually a magificent tool for perfect learning. It is completely impersonal. . . ."

In his insightful critique *Reincarnation—A Christian Appraisal*, Mark Albrecht casts some light on that assertion with this example:

Hitler died in 1945; let us suppose that he was reborn in 1947 as a crippled baby named Edgar Jones. Edgar, who was born in New York, has no idea that he is really Adolf Hitler reincarnated or that he is suffering for the crimes of the Nazi Fuhrer. It is at this point that justice breaks down totally, for the truth of the matter is that only Adolf Hitler can work off his karma and be punished for his evil deeds. But he is gone, since his personality actually ceased to exist in 1945, and little Edgar Jones now bears the massive burden of Hitler's karmic debt. Hitler thus cheats the hangman while Edgar is victimized. When Edgar dies, another person is born with Hitler's karma, and so the process is repeated millions of times...the bitter pill of this continual suffering would probably have a chain-reaction effect, causing bitterness and ill will to spread, perhaps even producing more Hitlers.

If there are those who are repelled by the idea of a God of judgment, surely they must reject all the more a god who judges *impersonally*—without justice, intelligence, empathy, or mercy. And make no mistake about it—if karma is what it is made out to be, it has all the attributes of a lesser god whose arms are too short to pick us up when we fall.

New Age reincarnationists proudly proclaim that there is no personal god outside of ourselves, but only an impersonal law by which we operate. I am curious as to how much they really enjoy being a mere face in the crowd, getting letters addressed to "occupant," being a social security number on a computer printout, or talking to answering machines!

Maybe it takes a lawyer to fully appreciate how cold and impersonal the law can sometimes be. Law is an inadequate peacemaker; it brings no reconciliation, no true satisfaction. When the boundary-dispute case has been decided in court, the neighbors still have to get along with each other. And no law can make that happen. The law of karma certainly will never be accused of great warmth or humanity.

By contrast, God knew well the limitations of law—any law. The God of the Bible, who originally gave the Laws of Moses, has now brought us grace and truth through the *person* of Jesus Christ. The law was never intended by God to bring reconciliation and salvation. Rather, God intended the law to show us how sinful we are, how in need we are of his grace.

The God of the Bible does not wait for us to work out our karmic debt before he judges us eligible for salvation; he bases our eligibility on the sacrifice of his Son in our place:

> When we were still powerless, Christ died for the ungodly. . . . God demonstrates his own love for us in this: While we were still sinners, Christ died for us. Since we have now been justified by his blood, how much more shall we be saved from God's wrath through him! (Romans 5:6,8,9).

ᴧ

KARMA'S DOUBLE STANDARD

It is always frustrating to deal with a double standard. Yet that is what we face in the alternative authority systems offered to us. On one hand we are told that karma dictates who and what we will be in our future lives, all based impartially on the law of cause and effect. On the other hand, Shirley MacLaine tells us that we ourselves make those decisions. That's confusing enough, but the implication is worse.

By whose standard are we being judged? Karma's or our own? Again, on one hand we are told that if we don't "get it right" by karma's standards, we face a disappointing reassignment the next time around. On the other hand we are told that we should act upon the truth which Ms. MacLaine says is within ourselves, as we come to know it through our unique insight and experiences. Is that obvious conflict fair? We would feel that an injustice had been done if parents were to tell a child to do whatever he thinks is right while they are gone for the evening, but then, when they discover he has eaten five bowls of ice cream, scold him for not having better nutritional values.

The law of karma would not stand the slightest judicial scrutiny. As a matter of due process, the courts have insisted on clear definition and the giving of adequate notice in regulatory statutes. Vagrancy laws, for example, have repeatedly been held invalid for containing such broad language that they made illegal all sorts of harmless activity. If tested in the same way, the law of karma would not only be "void for vagueness," but it would also be struck down for providing *no standards whatever*!

I find it particularly amazing that fairness-minded Americans would believe in a system of judgment which is tied to *no knowable guidelines* for human conduct. There is no source of rules, patterns, or principles for karma that would be comparable, for example, to the Bible or other written moral codes.

What New Age karma says is: "Look within yourself and decide what you think you ought to be and to do in your life; then, when you die, it will be decided whether or not you made good choices. If you did *not* make good choices, then there is no alternative but to let you suffer the consequences which naturally follow from your poor choices."

Even our Constitution prohibits the passing of legislation which results in criminal liability *ex post facto*—i.e., after the fact. The purpose of the prohibition is to prevent the unfairness which results when someone is punished for doing an act without being given prior notice of its wrongfulness. Because karma gives us no notice of the causes whose effects we will have to suffer in future lives, it is *ex post facto* moral judgment.

One minute Ms. MacLaine insists that it is a bad thing to judge one's beliefs or actions. The next minute she says that everything is the result of karmic cause and effect, which is the ultimate, impersonal, inescapable moral judgment. But worse yet, it is a judgment without any clear moral standard to judge by.

Think about it: What *is* the standard we are to follow if not the teachings of the proven Word of God, the Bible? Is it "universal morality"? (Does everyone agree on the morals?) Is it "doing our own thing"? (Even to the detriment of others?) Is it following our own conscience? (Are you prepared to give that option to your local neighborhood gang leader?) Is it meeting society's expectations? (Which society's? The Ayatollah's?) Is it rigorous attention to diets, exercise, and meditation? (Can we ever diet enough, exercise enough, or meditate enough?) Is it our feelings? (On what day?) Is it our experiences? (At what point in our lives?)

Any of those standards leaves too much leeway for questionable conduct and situational ethics. On what basis could we ever, as a society, make necessary social judgments about anyone else's conduct? Who could become a legislator, judge, or law-enforcer? Doesn't one person's enlightenment become another person's bad karma? Doesn't it put a premium on our choice of which standard to follow? Suppose we are wrong in the very *standard* we choose?

FAILING AT PERFECTION

Even if we could discover which standard the law of karma was going to judge us by, we would then be faced with the task of *living up to* that standard—on our own effort. And it is futile to try to reach perfection on our own: We know we can never do it in a single lifetime, and there is no reason to believe we could do it over a million lifetimes. Time doesn't solve problems inherent within the system.

The most basic of all bad karma, we are told, is the mere belief in the reality of life itself. Therefore people who *think* they have been born into this world, and *think* they live in this material world as we perceive it to be, are automatically destined to come back again in order to realize that it is nothing but illusion—which in itself is an odd way to help someone see reality! So it is impossible to either live up to a perfect standard of conduct (itself an unknown) or to rid ourselves of the great illusion.

Realizing that the *Titanic* of reincarnation has collided with that cold fact and is going down fast, the Western reincarnationists unashamedly jump into lifeboats marked "For Christians Only." Remember that the captain of the ship was just telling the passengers how seaworthy the law of karma is, because it is absolutely impersonal and always dispenses out cause and effect to keep the keel of life perfectly centered and balanced. But as the lifeboats hit the water, you hear the reincarnationists talking about a new lifesaving method that no one back in the home port of Calcutta ever heard of. Once again, Van Auken speaks for the reincarnationists:

> Associated with these "quirks" in the law [of karma] is the most amazing aspect of the law, *grace*. Grace is like getting a temporary release from the law in order to get oneself back together. When a soul turns around from its self-oriented ways and begins to look again for its original purpose and first love, the law is *temporarily*

suspended. This gives the seeking soul time to gather its strength for the journey home. The soul will still have to meet itself and its thoughts, actions, and words along the way, but it will be up to the task because of grace.

Well, there we have it—the ultimate Christianization of karma! But it is also the ultimate *emasculation* of karma, because for centuries we have been told that karma's advantage over Christianity is that with karma nothing is left to chance, capriciousness, or any silly notions of mercy or forgiveness. What you do is what you get.

Now we are told that karma can be temporarily suspended. Of course, we are not told under what circumstances it *will* be suspended, or what it means to give "the seeking soul time to gather its strength for the journey home." Nor are we given the slightest clue as to where this law of grace was ever discovered in the cosmic order, or how it can possibly coexist with the mutually exclusive law of karma. Nevertheless, the New Age story is that, where bad karma abounds, Christian grace will abound too. Of course, this would make as much sense as the Soviet communists condemning capitalism then introducing free enterprise.

Karma is an impotent, impersonal, and uncaring god. Dressing it up in the unfamiliar garb of pseudochristian grace only makes it uncomfortable and totally bizarre. True, the closer the resemblance to the genuine, the more successful the fraud. But beneath that garb karma is still karma—impotent, impersonal, and uncaring.

TRUE CHRISTIAN GRACE

Christian grace is the free gift of God to all those who have committed their lives to him in faith. It has nothing to do with fulfillment of any law. In fact, Christian grace is necessary because no one *can* fulfill the law. It does not demand that we make ourselves perfect over many lifetimes. God's grace takes away our sin and regards us as perfect even when we are not. The apostle Paul was adamant in affirming that salvation is not accomplished by works, whether Christian or karmic: "By grace you have been saved, through faith—and this not from yourselves, it is the gift of God—not by works, so that no one can boast. For we are God's workmanship, created in Christ Jesus to do good works."

I recently stood in the room where the great hymn "Amazing Grace" was written by John Newton. The serenity of the second-floor study in the old vicarage at Olney, in Buckinghamshire, belied the stormy life that Newton had experienced. At the age of 23 Newton almost lost his life as a sailor on board a cargo ship tossing wildly in rough seas. When he called out to God above the sound of the raging wind, he was amazed at God's mercy in saving him. Yet it was not this experience alone that inspired the words of the world's most popular hymn.

During his time as a merchant marine, Newton had been involved in the African slave-trade. Guilt-ridden, he later renounced the practice. He became a minister and joined in the fight to abolish slavery. Had he been thinking solely of his close brush with death, the first verse of the hymn might have been: "Amazing grace, how sweet the sound, that saved me from the storm-tossed seas." But Newton realized that God's grace was far more significant than saving a life from death. He believed that by God's grace he had become a new man, a forgiven soul reborn.

Together with a small group of Christians gathered in Newton's study on a rainy day, I too knew the rich meaning of God's grace in my life. I felt what Newton must have felt when he looked back on his imperfect life and realized that God had offered free pardon from sins. And as we joyously sang the hymn with misty eyes and lumps in our throats, I thanked God.

> Amazing grace! how sweet the sound
> That saved a wretch like me!
> I once was lost but now am found,
> Was blind, but now I see.

> Yes, when this heart and flesh shall fail
> And mortal life shall cease,
> I shall possess within the veil
> A life of joy and peace.

If we are looking for someone who really cares about us and the struggles we encounter every day, it is *God* to whom we must turn. Karma couldn't care less.

CHAPTER ELEVEN

SO WHAT'S THE APPEAL?

"We adhere, as though to a raft, to those ideas which represent our understanding."

—JOHN KENNETH GALBRAITH
The Affluent Society

IF KARMA IS ACTUALLY UGLY and dangerous in the light of human experience and biblical truth, why does it look so good to so many people? One key to karma's popularity is quite simple: Karma purports to explain why bad things happen for no apparent reason. Ms. MacLaine and many others find a certain sense of satisfaction in believing that cause and effect are behind all the adversity we meet. And this relates to our feelings when prosperity comes our way, too. It's kind of a twin relationship—pat yourself on the back because blessings prove your worth, and blame the sins of your previous lives for any calamity.

When skies are rosy and everything is going well, most people borrow a line from "The Sound of Music": "Somewhere in my youth or childhood I must have done something good." But when circumstances become adverse, many of those same people will ask, "What did I ever do to deserve this?" Whether good times or bad, people look for a cause-effect relationship.

When times are good, we like to assume that it is because

we have been living right. There's a certain sense of ego involved, as if we through our own goodness deserve good things to happen to us.

Yet if we insist on attributing our good times to our own righteous living or moral effort, then we naturally assume that the opposite is true as well. Consistency demands that we attribute our *bad* times to our own unrighteous living or moral failure. We tend to forget the fact that, just as good things can happen to bad people, bad things can also happen to good people without any adverse implication about their goodness.

At the point of tragedy we can blame God, blame ourselves, or come up with an alternative explanation. Some choose to blame God, and they "lose their faith" overnight. Some blame God in a secondary sense, like the popular Rabbi Kushman, who says that bad things happen to good people because God isn't powerful enough to stop them from happening. For most others, there is an almost intuitive understanding that God is a loving God who does not send suffering our way. So that leaves *ourselves* to blame. Yet that is often where we run into a brick wall. Either we are unwilling to admit our faults or else we realize our faults but can't understand how they could possibly be so serious as to merit some great tragedy in our lives.

SHIFTING THE BLAME

Karma offers an alternative explanation. It keeps the blame on us, but one giant step removed. It says that we are responsible, but not in this lifetime. It says that what we are experiencing is the result of what we have done in previous lives. Our tragedy is simply part of a cosmic system of higher education.

For many people karma is an alluring explanation because it shifts any immediate blame to past lives we can't even remember. We're responsible for bad things that happen to us, but we don't have to feel guilty about it. It's also captivating because it is *something* to hang onto, even if there's not an ounce of truth to it. At least it is *some* explanation, which for many people is better than no explanation at all.

But there are two serious problems with karma's explanation. The first is simply that, as we have already seen, none of us has ever had a prior life in which to accumulate bad karma. The second problem is that, while we *can* be the cause of our own suffering, we are not always *necessarily* the cause.

Remember hearing about the patience of Job? Job, of course, was the biblical figure who is known for the great suffering he endured. He was once a rich man who lost everything he had, including his family and his own health. His story, found in the book of Job, describes how he came to grips with the cause of his suffering. There's an important message for us in what he learned. When Job experienced great suffering, his friends repeatedly insisted that it was the result of sin. When Job protested, they assured him all the more that he was undoubtedly covering up some sin that had caused his misery. But the message that God communicated to Job is that there is not necessarily a connection between sin and suffering, or righteousness and prosperity. Karma, the book of Job tells us, is simply not an adequate explanation.

That is also Jesus' teaching. Neither Kevin nor David ever told Ms. MacLaine what Jesus really had to say. On one occasion Jesus squarely addressed the issue when he was told about the Galileans who had been attacked and killed by Roman soldiers as they were busy sacrificing in the temple: "Do you think that these Galileans were worse sinners than all the other Galileans because they suffered this way?" Jesus asked. "I tell you, no!"

Then, to emphasize the fact that there is no karmic cause-and-effect relationship between sin and suffering, Jesus brought up still another tragedy with which they were familiar. "Or those eighteen who died when the tower in Siloam fell on them—do you think they were more guilty than all the others living in Jerusalem? I tell you, no!"

Jesus taught vigorously against karmic notions, some of which can even interfere with the right attitude in personal relationships. "You have heard that it was said, 'Eye for eye, and tooth for tooth.' But I tell you, Do not resist an evil person. If someone strikes you on the right cheek, turn to him the other also." The eye-for-an-eye concept is like a first cousin to karma. Jesus said that we must learn to overcome any such attitudes.

Our example comes from God himself. Jesus reminds us: "He causes his sun to rise on the evil and the good, and sends rain on the righteous and the unrighteous." Not even the weather is karmic. If one farmer suffers from a drought, it says nothing bad about the kind of life he is living. If another farmer gets all the rain he needs, that gives him no reason to think he has a direct line to God.

We all know people who have an instant answer for everything, whether or not they know what they are talking about. We say of them: "Often wrong, but never in doubt." When offered as an explanation for things that go wrong, karma is like that. Karma may be an *easy* explanation, but it is certainly not the *right* explanation.

✸

NO ORIGINAL CAUSE-AND-EFFECT

Many people are comfortable with cause-and-effect spiritual explanations because of the widely accepted idea that at the time we are born we are somehow already loaded down with sin. So when the law of karma says that each person begins his or her life with a certain amount of bad karma to work off, the idea is not radically new to Western ears.

Jesus taught an important lesson when he said that we must become like little children: "I tell you the truth, unless you change and become like little children, you will never enter the kingdom of heaven. . .for the kingdom of God belongs to such as these." Why would Jesus tell us that we must become like children if they are condemned with sin or bad karma?

We are not working out *anyone's* sin or bad karma—not our parents' and certainly not our own from any previous lives. What we *are* working out is our own sinful nature in this life that part of ourselves about which we are morally embarrassed; that darker side of us that perhaps even our closest friends don't know about; that part of our spiritual selves that we wish we could change.

Under the law of karma, as it is universally explained, we stand always condemned, even from birth. But as Christians we have an escape from such a harsh law of cause-and-effect, whether it be the contrived law of karma or the law of sin and death referred to in the Bible. Ms. MacLaine's spiritual mentors never told her about it, and you can't find it in any of the books supporting karma or reincarnation. But the

Bible makes a most wonderful promise—to you, to me, to Shirley MacLaine, and to anyone else who will accept the teaching:

> Therefore, there is now *no condemnation* for those who are in Christ Jesus, because through Christ Jesus the law of the Spirit of life *set me free from the law of sin and death* (Romans 8:1,2).

Can anything be more reassuring? Is any idea more liberating? In Christ I am set free from the law of sin and death. In Christ I am set free from the law of cause-and-effect. In Christ I am set free from any claimed law of karma. As a Christian I am no longer condemned, and *that* is a promise which is worth going out on a limb to believe!

EXPLAINING THE SUFFERING?

Apart from human suffering, the idea of karma would never have been conceived. Suffering needed an explanation, and karma seemed to fill the bill. But is it a good explanation? Ms. MacLaine was initially intrigued by the thought that it might be. "How," she asked herself, "did you reconcile the injustice of the accident of birth into poverty and deprivation when others were born into comfort? Was life really that cruel? Was life simply an accident?"

When David suggested that there are no accidents—that behind everything is a higher purpose, Ms. MacLaine realized that some pretty heavy implications are involved. "I wonder how six million dead Jews feel about being part of a higher conscious cosmic design," she demanded, almost angrily. And David had to agree that no one has good answers for such atrocities.

It is too easy to offer the simplistic law of karma as the answer to the profound question of human suffering—and an unloving, cruel hoax on those who desperately search for answers.

Although I have not personally experienced truly intense suffering, I have seen the faces of suffering. I have watched as a favorite uncle wasted away in the agony of cancer. In Iquitos, Peru, I've seen the poverty of little four-year-old Roberto reflected in his eyes. I've seen the tension of those who live each day in Northern Ireland, and of those who walk the streets of Londonderry, not knowing if the car they are passing will blow up in their faces. I walked in the dusty marketplace of Addis Abba, Ethiopia, just days before the coup that killed Haile Selasie, and saw there the despair on the faces of merchants who had gone without business for weeks and months. In my work as a District Attorney I was shocked at the sight of a six-month-old baby, abused and abandoned, with cigarette burns over her emaciated body.

I can tell you that the happiest day of my life as a lawyer was the day I was able to take a child forever out of her parents' custody. She was nine years old and as cute as she could be. When the school nurse asked her about the bruises she had observed, of course the little girl said they had come from a fall.

We later learned from her father that he had beaten her—repeatedly—with a paddle made in shop class by one of the girl's older brothers. The physical abuse was the least of it. At Christmas the other children got new bicycles, but she had gotten nothing. Why? What had brought on her suffering? "The wife and I wanted our other children," the father freely admitted, "but we never wanted *this* one!"

No, I don't relate to intense suffering in a personal sense, but I do appreciate how real it is to other people. And I admit that I don't have all the answers to the "why" of suffering. But I do know that God has the *solution* to suffering: his eternal purpose in Christ Jesus.

In much of the world's suffering we have no cause to blame past-life karma, but only our own irresponsibility. Thus we are rarely in a good position to raise the often-asked question as to why God permits evil to exist in the world. We ourselves are too often the ones who permit it! The person who drives while intoxicated one night is in no position to ask God why he permitted the death of a child by a reckless driver the next night. Those of us who go through ghetto areas on our way to a football game and never stop to consider what we might do to relieve ghetto misery are in no position to ask why God allows people to suffer in Ethiopia. Until *we* have done all that we can do to stop governments from sending young men to their deaths on foreign soils, we are in no position to ask why God permits other suffering which we can't directly link to our personal irresponsibility and sin.

Yet there is a different kind of suffering which cannot be attributed to anyone in this life. The examples we inevitably turn to are the children who have been born with physical or mental handicaps. Apart from the cases which have resulted from known hereditary causes or medical malpractice, there seems to be little explanation for such tragedies, if you discount the insensitive karmic explanation offered by the reincarnation philosophy which Ms. MacLaine advocates.

When Ms. MacLaine says that there is a karmic reason for everything bad that happens to us, she is only adding to the suffering. Imagine what guilt a person feels when you convince him that he was not simply an unfortunate victim of child abuse when he was young, but that he himself was responsible for it. Ms. MacLaine is not contributing to a healthy, positive outlook on life when she adamantly insists that everyone is participating at every moment in everything that happens to him or her.

By our very humanness our present understanding is limited and incomplete. However, I firmly believe that in the life to come we *will* understand suffering, pain, and evil. And I believe that, seen from God's perspective, there is an answer which we will all accept without the slightest hesitation.

❧

ONE THING WE CAN KNOW

If we don't have all the answers we would like, this one thing we *can* know: There is a personal God, outside our human situation, who cares about suffering. I say "outside our situation" to emphasize that God is *distinct and separate from his creation* and not a part of the evil we experience. When Ms. MacLaine's spiritual mentors insist that all is One—that we and God and everything in the universe are all One—that can only mean that *evil is also One*, and therefore that God is evil. Whatever else may be said, you can count on this fact above all others: God is not evil.

God is love.

While there is not a hint that karma has the capacity to care—really care—about what happens to us, the God of the Bible sent his only Son into *our* world to experience *our* suffering. Jesus was despised and rejected. He was "a man of sorrows, and familiar with suffering." In his sacrificial death, he was "oppressed and afflicted." When nailed to the cross, "he was pierced for our transgressions, he was crushed for our iniquities."

As a fellow sufferer, Jesus knew what he was saying when he promised: "Blessed are you who are poor, for yours is the kingdom of God. Blessed are you who hunger now, for you will be satisfied. Blessed are you who weep now, for you will laugh."

While the concept of karma is powerless to intervene and stop the endless cycle of suffering and death over which it supposedly has control, God has decreed that there will be an end to the cycle. He has prepared a life after this life in which the present suffering will fade into nothingness. As Paul told the Roman Christians: "I consider that our present sufferings are not worth comparing with the glory that will be revealed in us."

What kind of glory can God's people look forward to in the life to come? "He will wipe every tear from their eyes. There will be no more death or mourning or crying or pain, for the old order of things has passed away."

In the world to come for those who believe in reincarnation, there is only more disease, more destruction, and more death. In the world to come for the children of God, there will be no more suffering, and the lion will lie down at peace with the lamb.

WHAT KIND OF MOTIVATION?

For Shirley MacLaine, karma is also attractive because of the *motivation* it provides.

...it's strange, but knowing that there is a law of cause and effect in operation makes me very aware of how precious every single moment of every single day can be.... Nothing—literally—nothing is insignificant. Every thought, every gesture, everything I say and do, has an energy attached to it which is positive.... I'm aware that everything has a reason for happening. Also, I know that whatever good I can do, whatever fun I can share, whatever contribution I make, even if it's to say "Good morning!" to someone, will somewhere, sometime, come back to me. It's not a matter of making Brownie points. It just feels a... lot better in *me*.

But Ms. MacLaine's "high motivation" doesn't translate well to the majority of reincarnationists. To begin with, since when has any *law* been the highest form of motivation? Don't we often take law as a challenge to find some way around it or as an excuse to ignore it?

Second, karmic law and successive incarnations actually are more of a motivator for complacency and irresponsibility in this lifetime. Given the prospect of many chances, and an *inevitable* absorption of every soul into the Divine Consciousness, there would seem to be no compelling rush to "get it right." It is unavoidable that many people who accept reincarnation will take on an attitude of cosmic complacency.

Reincarnation could be defined as wishful thinking about the soul's resurrection, for which one is not ready. You can almost hear someone say, "I *want* to believe that I have many lifetimes, because I am not prepared to face the alternative. If I accept the message of the Bible, I know that when this life is over, I get no second chances. I will be judged solely on the basis of what I have done about the lordship of Jesus Christ. If given the choice, I much prefer to 'meet myself' when I die than to 'meet my Maker.' "

Ms. MacLaine's friend, Gerry, saw the problem when Shirley first mentioned her fascination with reincarnation. Referring to those who are in cultures where reincarnation is the prevalent belief, Gerry observed:

> I mean, they don't tend to their lives as though they could improve them. I mean, they just exist as though it will be better the next time around, and this time isn't all that important.

A reincarnationist may answer that, the longer we wait, the more karmic debt we will accumulate. But even this doesn't seem to matter on the cosmic scale of things. Despite the practical impossibility of anyone working off his karmic debt, the way reincarnation is presented, everyone is going to "get it right" eventually in any event.

The reason there is no concept of hell in the theory of reincarnation is that (at least ideally) each successive life is on a higher level of spiritual evolution. Sure, in your next life you may be born with a physical handicap for what you do wrong in this lifetime, but it's all a process of growth, and everyone will eventually make it. Regardless of how you live today, *someday* you'll get your act together and it will all work out.

So *everybody wins*, including the guy at the office who cheated you out of a promotion, the parent who may have sexually abused you, and the spouse who left you for somebody else. That's right, *everybody wins*—even Attila the Hun, Adolf Hitler, Idi Amin, Colonel Gaddafi, and the Ayatollah Khomeini. Granted, they may be in the last wave, pulling up the rear, but, as they come across the finish line, everyone will be waiting there to cheer them on. *With reincarnation, nobody loses!* No wonder the idea of reincarnation sounds appealing!

✦

THE MYTH OF EVOLUTION

Reincarnation's basic concept of spiritual evolution is comfortable to a lot of people because they already believe in biological evolution of the physical human species. The widely accepted belief in amoeba-to-man evolution makes it easy for a person to be convinced that there might also be evolution of the soul. Yet in *Dancing in the Light*, Ms. MacLaine raised an important point when she considered the relationship between body evolution and soul evolution:

> As I lay in the tub thinking, I wondered how long it would be before scientists would find ways to verify the evolution of the soul in the same way that they have verified the evolution of the body.

But first things first. How well *have* the scientists verified evolution of the body? Imagine my surprise to see that the discovery of the world's greatest fraud has surfaced in, of all places, *The Aquarian Conspiracy*, the handbook of New Age thinking! While maintaining an unquestioned alliance with the idea of evolution and insisting that we are at the threshold of still another great evolutionary leap, author Marilyn Ferguson makes a major concession regarding Darwinian evolution:

Darwin's theory of evolution by chance mutation and survival of the fittest has proven hopelessly inadequate to account for a great many observations in biology. . . . Darwin ignored problems in his own evidence. True, there seemed to be great gaps, missing rungs in the ladder of evolution, but he believed these were just imperfections in the geological record. Change only *seemed* abrupt. *But to this day fossil evidence has not turned up the necessary missing links* [Emphasis added].

Citing no less an authority than Harvard biologist and geologist Steven Jay Gould, Ferguson notes:

Gould called the extreme rarity in the fossil record of transitional forms of life "the trade secret of paleontology." Younger scientists, confronted by the continuing absence of such missing links, are increasingly skeptical of the old theory. "The old explanation that the fossil record was inadequate is in itself an inadequate explanation," said Niles Eldredge of the American Museum of Natural History.

In just the last 20 years, we have come a long way from "proof" of evolution which was said to be "unchallengeable" to recognition that Darwinian evolution never was a valid explanation to begin with. To be sure, even though they are otherwise at a loss to explain how the process took place, and even though they are hopelessly divided regarding what actually happened, most scientists still believe that man somehow resulted from chance biological forces. And even while prominent scientists are finally coming out of the closet to admit that Darwin's hoped-for evidence has never been found, many who call themselves Christians are still trying to appear hip, believing that they can reconcile the irreconcilable through some form of theistic evolution.

✦

THE FATAL FLAW

The truth is that the basic concept is fatally flawed, and the general public would be amazed if all the cards were ever put on the table honestly. But that is another book altogether. Suffice it to say in this context that, on the testimony of even secular scientists, Darwin's celebrated theory of evolution has finally been exposed as the Big Lie of the nineteenth and twentieth centuries.

As one of millions who still believe in the Big Lie, Ms. MacLaine insists that there is evolution of the spirit just as there is evolution of the body. But in attempting to reconcile her belief in reincarnation with her belief in evolution, Ms. MacLaine creates a thorny problem for herself. If evolution is correct, where do we get a "spirit," "soul," or "cosmic entity" to begin with? Before something can evolve, it has to *be*. In the naturalistic, materialistic, biological concept of evolution, there is no room whatever for the metaphysical concept of soul or spirit. Evolution does not even attempt to explain, nor could it explain, the existence of the spiritual entity which each one of us is. In fact, over the last century the notion of evolution has been a major contributing factor to our *lack* of a spiritual dimension. Evolution has been telling us through every medium imaginable that we are *only* biological, *only* natural, *only* physical phenomena. We are body and mind, yes, but *not spirit*.

Isn't that where Shirley MacLaine and I came in? Isn't that the starting point upon which we both agree? What we are both trying to show is that we are spirit as well! *Primarily* spirit! Yet it is clear that spirit and evolution have been enemies from the day they met.

Assume for a moment that there had been some external creation of the soul apart from evolution. At what point did souls start entering into physical bodies? And what *were* those earthly packages? Adam? Near-Adam? Almost-nearly-Adam? The last ape before almost-nearly-Adam? Incredibly, in an effort to reconcile her belief in the immortal human soul with her belief in biological evolution, that is exactly where Shirley MacLaine takes us. In *Dancing in the Light*, Ms. MacLaine tells us that souls were created before the world began and then "eventually. . . souls lodged in evolved primates that later became Homo sapiens."

So there we have it: Shirley MacLaine puts the immortal human soul into the body of an ape. Has she stopped to consider the implication of that conclusion? It means that many (if not all) of *us* once had the body of an ape or perhaps even a fish or an amoeba! Sure, due to our advanced body evolution (we are told) we don't transmigrate *back* into lower life forms these days, but the fact remains that, if Ms. MacLaine is right about cosmic history, *we were once souls within apes!*

It is amazing enough that people are willing to believe that their *bodies* somehow descended from apes, but I don't think many people have stopped to think that *their own souls* were inside those beastly creatures! And I doubt if many psychics are including previous primate incarnations in their trendy metaphysical counseling. Apart from simply being a degrading idea, primate incarnations would surely

SO WHAT'S THE APPEAL?

have serious repercussions regarding alleged human karma and speculative karmic relationships. The practical problems are endless. Ms. MacLaine's effort to crusade for greater spiritual awareness while holding onto a belief in biological evolution merely broadsides her own cause.

✦

BACK TO THE TRUE CREATOR

Why do we insist on fanciful explanations of our origin which collapse under the bones of each discarded scientific theory? The Genesis account of creation is not just a legend or a narrow-minded religionist notion. "In the beginning God created the heavens and the earth" is still the most comprehensive and best-documented explanation of our existence. And it is the only view which is consistent with Christian teaching. Christ was not simply the living Word of God who appeared for a time in human form on this earth. Jesus Christ, God in the flesh, was himself the *Creator*. John (referring to Jesus Christ as the Word) begins his Gospel account with that grand affirmation:

> In the beginning was the Word, and the Word was with God, and the Word was God. He was with God in the beginning.
> Through him all things were made; without him nothing was made that has been made.

If Christ was not our Creator, then neither is he our Savior.

Evolution has darkened our understanding by drawing a curtain between the universe and ourselves. A sense of mystery and awe has been replaced by hypothesis and speculation. By dethroning the God of creation, reducing human existence to spiritless materialism, and deceiving us about the very nature and purpose of our lives on this earth, the idea of evolution has set back for over a century the spiritual understanding of mankind.

Who can possibly ignore the vastly different views of our spiritual nature that each perspective presents? Ms. MacLaine's belief system says that man's spirit emanated from the God Source, somehow found its way into the body of a primate and, through a progression of slowly evolving subhuman bodies, eventually manifested in human form, having been shaped and influenced by its previous sub-human existence. By contrast, through the majesty of the Genesis account we are told that—

> the Lord God formed man from the dust of the ground and breathed into his nostrils the breath of life, and man became a living being.

✦

ORIGIN, PURPOSE, DESTINY

In any discussion of life's meaning, the formula of inquiry has always been: *origin*, purpose, and destiny. You can't know where you are and where you are going unless you know where you've come from. The Bible itself begins with origins, then explores the meaning of earthly existence, and concludes with our eternal destiny. The reclaiming of God's creation in the final book, Revelation, makes no sense without the *fact of creation* and the spiritual fall of *created man*, as told in the opening pages of Genesis.

Throughout the entire Bible, God's creation of man—body

and soul—is at the very heart of the matter. The apostle Paul put the explanation of our origin and purpose into sharp focus when he addressed the philosophers at the acropolis in Athens:

> The God who made the world and everything in it is the Lord of heaven and earth and does not live in temples built by hands. And he is not served by human hands, as if he needed anything, because he himself gives all men life and breath and everything else. From one man he made every nation of men, that they should inhabit the whole earth; and he determined the times set for them and the exact places where they should live.
>
> God did this so that men would seek him and perhaps reach out for him and find him, though he is not far from each one of us. "For in him we live and move and have our being." As some of your own poets have said, "We are his offspring" (Acts 17:24-28).

Regarding our spiritual nature, there are no more sublime words in all of divine revelation than these:

> God created man in his own image, in the image of God he created him; male and female he created them (Genesis 1:27).

Neither our bodies nor our souls are the product of chance existence or evolutionary struggle. Having ordained one lifetime for each person, God has put us into this world with dignity, honor, and divine purpose. We are the crowning glory of his creation!

Our greatest need is to catch the vision that mankind has been purposefully, intelligently, and spontaneously brought into existence by the Creator of the universe—in his very likeness—and to sense the value and spiritual potential that each individual thereby represents.

Ideas have consequences. If we are of the earth, beastlike, then we will think of ourselves as beastly, and we will act like beasts. If we are of heaven, Godlike, then we will think of ourselves as godly, and we will act like God would act.

✦

THE CYNIC'S MISTAKE

Why has reincarnation caught on so readily in Western societies? I have the uneasy feeling that many people are turning to a belief in reincarnation only by default. For the unchurched, it provides a rationale for one's existence. Everyone has to believe in *something*. Somewhere along the line, each person must decide where he came from, why he is here, and what he thinks will happen to him after he dies. For many people, therefore, reincarnation is a substitute for traditional, organized religion.

All throughout the New Age and Westernized reincarnation literature is a very noticeable undercurrent of bitterness about "the church." "The church," so it is said, has deceived and misled people, selfishly interpreted the Scriptures, wrongfully asserted its power, and become the cause of all the problems in the world. Because of "the church," we no longer have the Scriptures in their original form. Because of "the church" we are not aware of the missing years in Jesus' life. Because of "the church" we have been kept from knowing about cosmic truth, human potential, and self-enlightenment.

"The church" being referred to is not always clearly defined. Most of the references which Ms. MacLaine and her friends made to "the church" were references to the Roman Catholic Church, particularly with regard to the historical alterations which they allege came at the hands of various Church councils. At other times, however, they were referring with disdain to all institutionalized, dogmatized, hierarchical, and traditional churches in general.

Even as a Christian, I agree with some of their criticisms. In "the church" as it is viewed generally, there are ritualistic and spiritually dead churches which masquerade as the body of Christ on earth. There are pulpit-pounders, television beggars, egocentric entertainers, and preachers of pious sweet-nothings all across the country. Little wonder that some people run confused into the arms of atheism, agnosticism, humanism, or even reincarnation.

If anyone has reason to be cynical about "the church" and the many divisions which constantly plague it, I do. One of my most vivid memories, as a boy of 11, was the scene in my home one Sunday afternoon when some of the members of our church came by to console my father, who had just been fired because of what he had preached from the pulpit that morning (over an issue which is by no means at the heart of Christian teaching). As the result of a hastily called meeting, my father was not even permitted to speak at the evening service. It was the first time I remember seeing my father cry. You can imagine the impact on an 11-year-old whose primary interest was in trading bubblegum baseball cards and playing outfield for the Washington Senators.

I understand about imperfect churches filled with imperfect people, both as an observer and as a church member.

I too have a long way to go in order to be the man of God that I ought to be. In view of the picture of Christ which we Christians often paint, Ms. MacLaine's early disenchantment with organized religion is not altogether surprising.

But there is reason for optimism amid all this discouragement. I see more and more people who are discovering the divine Person of Jesus Christ—not simply the security blanket of religious institutions. I see people starting to read the Bible for themselves—not just blindly following traditions and church creeds. I see that the fastest-growing churches today are local fellowships—not tied to hierarchical organizations, but autonomous in their search for New Testament Christianity. I see people getting up out of their comfortable pews and beginning to get a sense of sacrifice and service.

I even see Christians becoming more *spirit-minded*. Like Shirley MacLaine, they have had enough of materialistic Christianity and empty formalism. More and more people are discovering the joy of real spiritual commitment and a personal relationship with Christ. In their mutually-supportive local fellowships they are experiencing the truth of the Bible that God is knowable and approachable through our personal submission to the lordship of Jesus Christ.

It is *Christ* to whom we must look. Focusing on "the church" with all its human imperfection will often disappoint and disenchant us. Cynicism about "the church" is a misleading roadblock that somebody put up in the middle of the night. On the other side of cynicism is a clearer view of Christians who are on the road to spiritual maturity, walking in the light of Christ.

CHAPTER TWELVE
ME, MYSELF, AND I

"A man who bows down to nothing can never bear the burden of himself."

—FEODOR DOSTOEVSKI
A Raw Youth

THERE IS AN ODD SORT OF INCONSISTENCY in the way New Age thought is embraced by Ms. MacLaine. This philosophy says that all truth and meaning is found within the self. While on the one hand Ms. MacLaine's philosophy tells her that all truth is in herself, and that fulfillment will be found within, on the other hand she directed her spiritual odyssey primarily to external sources. It is an inconsistency that the Christian avoids by looking only to Jesus Christ for spiritual guidance. In looking for truth and meaning, Ms. MacLaine turned to the very source of her emptiness—herself.

"So this book is about a quest for myself—" Ms. MacLaine told us in the first chapter of *Out on a Limb*. And as she traveled and talked to people, the tone of their conversations "shifted from dismay and confusion to a consideration that the answers might lie within ourselves." David assured her that she was right. "*You* are everything," he told her. "Everything you want to know is inside of you. You are the universe." As Ms. MacLaine read the Edgar Cayce materials she was convinced that "the morality of their message was unmistakable. And a good set of values to live by. 'All the answers are within yourself,' they said. 'Only look.' "

I confess I am confused by what Ms. MacLaine proceeded to do after reaching that conclusion. Convinced that the answers were within herself, she spent months reading a virtual library of books, asking friends for *their* insight, and seeking out mediums who promised to put her in touch with cosmic truth found in a type of channeled revelation from supposed omniscient sources. If truth was *within herself* all along, why was all that external spiritual guidance necessary?

Saying that each of us must take responsibility for developing our own understanding and for evaluating what we are taught by others is a long way from declaring, "You are everything. Everything you want to know is inside of you. You are the universe."

Jesus identified the source of truth as *outside of one's self* and instead in an objective, knowable revelation of the mind of God: "If you hold to *my teaching*, you are really my disciples. Then you will know the truth, and the truth will set you free."

🟐

MAKING SELF GOD

The heart and soul of the New Age movement, which Ms. MacLaine embraces along with her reincarnation ideas, is nothing less than *self-deification*. Cayce follower Gina Cerminara derides as "a psychological crime" the thought that anyone should be saved through the sacrificial death of Christ. "It is a psychological crime because it places responsibility for redemption on something external to the self; it makes salvation dependent on belief in the divinity of another person rather than on self-transformation through belief in one's own intrinsic divinity."

If there were ever any doubt about what is being said, Kevin's channeled entity, "John," puts an end to any speculation:

> "So you mean if I'm to understand what this God thing is, I must know myself?" [Shirley asked.] "Correct," said John; "your soul is a metaphor for God."

Even Ms. MacLaine was struck with the full implication of that statement: "Well, I could become very arrogant if I really believed *I* was a metaphor for God."

John's response was but a further affirmation: "Never confuse the path you take with the truth itself." And there was more. John told Ms. MacLaine that the self "knows the Divine truth because the self is itself Divine." Is that close enough to self-deification? If not, here's the clincher:

> The skeptic's view of higher knowledge of self is most limiting. Your dogmatic religions, for example, are most limiting for mankind because they demand unquestioned reverence for authority —an exterior authority. *You* are God. *You* know you are Divine.

There it is in black and white, right there in *Out on a Limb.* Shirley MacLaine has just been made the propagator of me-generation self-worship!

But it really shouldn't be all that surprising. All we had

to do was put the equation together: We are One; God is One; therefore, we are God. The cosmic conjugation is: I am God, you are God, we are God.

In contrast, the Bible says that we are made in God's image as moral, intelligent, eternally-minded human beings who have been given dominion over the earth. When we commit our lives to Christ we become children of God by faith in Christ Jesus, heirs according to the promise, sons of God, and children of light.

If there was any lingering doubt in Ms. MacLaine's mind about her own self being a metaphor for God, in *Dancing in the Light* she quite clearly has resolved it in favor of self-deity. Her attempt at a logical syllogism is not only patently illogical but also brazenly blasphemous:

> I *know* that I exist, therefore I AM.
> I *know* that the God source exists. Therefore IT IS.
> Since I am a part of that force, then I AM that I AM.

Just in case the significance of that last phrase is lost on anyone, it should be pointed out that "I AM that I AM" is a biblical reference applied exclusivley to the Creator God of the universe, the one true and living God.

What Ms. MacLaine's higher self tells her (her H.S., as she abbreviates it) confirms what she wants to believe:

> "Then what is the difference between you and God?" [Shirley] asked [her higher self]. "None," it said. "I am God, because all energy is plugged in to the same source. We are each aspects of that source. We are all part of God. We are all

individualized reflections of the God source. God is us and we are God." "And *you* are me." "Precisely."

It is not just coincidence that Shirley MacLaine has accepted her own deity with ever-growing resolve. After all, she takes the first five minutes every day reminding herself that she is God. As she explains in *Dancing in the Light*, her daily affirmations make her feel good.

> Affirmations are spoken resolutions which, when used properly, align the physical, mental, and spiritual energies. The ancient Hindu vedas claimed that the spoken words *I am*, or *Aum* in Hindi, set up a vibrational frequency in the body and mind which align the individual with his or her higher self and thus with the God-source. The word God in any language carries the highest vibrational frequency of any word in the language. Therefore, if one says audibly *I am God*, the sound vibrations literally align the energies of the body to a higher atunement.
>
> You can use *I am God* or *I am that I am* as Christ often did, or you can extend the affirmation to fit your own needs.

Surely if someone tells herself repeatedly that she is God, it won't be long before she actually believes it!

THE ULTIMATE EGO TRIP

Telling ourselves that we are God is an expression of brazen pride. It puts us in the company of the original usurper, Satan, and also the ancient King of Tyre, of whom the prophet Ezekiel wrote:

> In the pride of your heart you say, "I am a god; I sit on the throne of a god in the heart of the seas." But you are a man and not a god, though you think you are as wise as a god.

Theologian Helmut Thielicke saw this kind of New Age presumptuousness for what it is: "The ultimate refinement of blasphemy, for it sets God in analogy to man."

Ms. MacLaine learned the message of self-deification from many sources. In virtually everything she read, her attention was focused on "the fact that so much of the message seemed to be universal—that is, entities channeling through a variety of people in many countries in different languages were saying basically the same thing. Look into yourselves, explore yourselves, *you* are the Universe...."

Actually the message is even more ancient and widespread than Ms. MacLaine may realize. The same message has been around since the Garden of Eden, when it was first subtly suggested by the Serpent, "You too can be God."

If we are really God, why can't we prevent our own deaths? Why can't we tell the law of karma to take a hike? Why can't we eliminate the suffering we now blame God for allowing? Why aren't we already supremely enlightened?

There's a certain headiness in the human accomplishments of our time. After all, we've been to the moon. We didn't *make* the moon, but we *have* managed to make a couple of brief visits there. Our attitude is not unlike two-year-olds who begin to discover what they can do—walking and talking and all sorts of wonderful new things. It is little wonder that, during the "terrible two's," the most-often-heard exclamation is, "*Me* do it!" In many ways, the "terrible two's" is an age we never seem to have outgrown.

It is an ongoing question of human sovereignty versus divine sovereignty. Are we ruled by theocracy, or are we ourselves an autocracy? The wise King Solomon had much to say about this personal referendum: "Trust in the Lord with all your heart and lean not on your own understanding. . . . Do not be wise in your own eyes. . . . There is a way that seems right to a man, but in the end it leads to death."

It is interesting that Ms. MacLaine and other New Agers point an accusing finger at materialism, yet are willing to elevate themselves to the status of godhood. Idolatry is defined as worshiping anything in this material world instead of the Creator who brought it into existence. Self-deification, as the ultimate idolatry, is therefore also the ultimate materialism. Most New Agers would think traditional idolatry—with wooden or metal gods—to be quite beneath their dignity. But in their new paradigm, wood and metal have only been replaced with flesh and blood.

While fancying themselves to be spiritualists, it is obvious that New Agers are, more accurately, *mentalists.* In her book *The Acquarian Conspiracy* (recognized as the most complete explanation of the New Age movement) Marilyn Ferguson asserts that their ultimate goal is the ability to achieve superconsciousness through the human mind, whether it be by meditation, yoga, biofeedback, music, chanting, hypnosis, "consciousness-raising," dream journals, psychotherapy, or mind-expanding drugs. The *mind* is seen as the door through which superlearning and self-enlightenment will come.

If superconsciousness is the goal, doesn't it make more sense to focus our attention on the omniscient, infinite mind of the One who had such a degree of superconsciousness that he could create *our* finite human minds? Otherwise we are restricting our own awareness by tapping into minds which can only question how they themselves work rather than into the creative Mind which already knows how they work. By establishing a personal relationship with the Creator himself, we are tapping into the infinite Mind of the universe.

✹

THE SECRET OF TRUE FULFILLMENT

New Age thinking can be faddish, chic, and trendy—something to talk about at cocktail parties. Yet the irony is that in many ways the New Age movement is only a return to ancient times—times of superstition, magic, and sorcery. When you think of the interest in astrology, tarot cards, psychic healers, and trance mediums, you can see the truth of what Solomon said: There is nothing new under the sun. Far from being progressive, the New Age movement is best characterized as *mass societal regression.*

We don't need regression into either witchcraft or fantasized past lives, but forward-looking optimism for a future not yet lived. Living in the past, whether through mysticism or psychoanalysis, is debilitating and wasteful. What's done is done, and we can't change it, whether it be birth into undesirable conditions, wasted youth, broken relationships, or presumed failures.

"Knowing yourself," as Ms. MacLaine was encouraged to do, can be a two-sided coin. I find that, if I look into the mirror too briefly, I quickly forget what I saw and need to look again. It's the same with people who spend little or no time taking measure of who and why they are. They live and die never knowing.

But if I look into the mirror too long, I see new wrinkles, less hair on top, and more gray in my beard. It's the same with people who become overly concerned with self. Their faults and needs are only exaggerated. They live anxiously and die of worry.

We need less awareness of our *selves*, and more awareness of *others*. We need to have less self-realization and more realization of the needs of others. Happiness is not being inward and selfish; happiness is being outward and sharing. It is being inwardly full so that you can share that fullness with others outwardly. Achieving happiness through otherness derives from the well-tested Christian principle that it is more blessed to give than to receive.

In showing us how to be truly fulfilled, Jesus taught that we need to lay down our lives for others—not to be more self-assertive. In order to fully live, we must die to our selves. Self-direction must be turned into self-denial. To find ourselves, we must lose ourselves. True self-actualization comes through giving up self to the lordship of Christ. When we are committed to loving and serving Christ and others, we will not be consumed by the void that eats at us when we are wrapped up in ourselves.

The quest for self begins with the assumption that something is *missing* in self. It is for this reason that self-deification becomes the Great Delusion. When that which is missing in our lives becomes the object of our worship, our god is reduced to an empty shell, and our self-worship is exposed as the Ultimate Folly.

CHAPTER THIRTEEN

STANDARDS OF A LESSER GOD

"We need not worry so much about what man descends from—it's what he descends to that shames the human race."

—ANONYMOUS

IF *POLITICS* MAKES STRANGE BEDFELLOWS, then *reincarnation* all the more—particularly "Christianized reincarnation." When the notion of reincarnation is applied practically to standards of morality and human conduct, traditional and biblical standards fall by the wayside. Christianity is made out to be a prehistoric relic, whose value-laden bones are picked clean by highly evolved karmic entities.

For example, through New Age reincarnation, homosexuality has taken on cosmic respectability. When "John" was being channeled through Kevin, he told Ms. MacLaine that she had been reincarnated twice as a male and once as a female. Shirley's curiosity was aroused when John said that everyone had experienced living as different sexes.

"Could that be a metaphysical explanation for homosexuality?" [Shirley asked.] "I mean, maybe a soul makes a rocky transition from a female to a male body, for instance, and there is left over emotional residue and attraction from the previous incarnation?" "As such," said John, affirmatively.

Edgar Cayce agreed, but indicated that homosexuality might be even more karmic. In one of the life readings given by Cayce, a young man with homosexual urges was told that he was a victim of boomerang karma. It seems that in a former life he had been a gossipmonger in the French court, and took particular delight in exposing homosexual scandals.

From the Cayce readings, Gina Cerminara tells us that there are also karmic aspects to adultery:

> In short, such cases would indicate that the infidelity of the mate sometimes occurs through karmic necessity. On the basis of these instances it cannot be assumed, of course, that *all* cases of infidelity are karmic. John's unfaithfulness to Mary may be due to the fact that Mary deserves this treatment because of her unfaithfulness to Claudius in ancient Rome, but on the other hand his philandering may stem from Mary's failing in the present; the infidelity may be no more than a contemporary reaction to a contemporary instigation— a case of quick karma.

Adultery may be just a karmic quickie? Try *that* one on your spouse! If he or she doesn't accept such a convenient cosmic excuse, and decides to file for divorce, then that's okay too, says Cerminara:

> Marriage as an institution is, by the reincarnationist view, less sacrosanct than many people

think. If society wishes to make marriage indissoluble, well and good; if not, again well and good. Cosmic law will not be thwarted by either system —if man fails to meet an obligation in one existence, he will irrevocably be called to task in another. The outer forms which man sets up are almost as arbitrary and almost as unimportant as the rules he devises for gin rummy.

So morality is just a matter of playing games. We can change the rules anytime we want to. If we want to change morality, we can do so by popular initiative, or legislation, or court rules, or church dogma, or altered societal attitudes. After all, nothing in this life really matters. It will all come out in the cosmic wash in another life.

THE KARMIC LINE OF REASONING

How far are we willing to take this line of reasoning? If we stick with the MacLaine-admired Cayce readings, we could come up with some very interesting situations. For example, there was the case of the woman whose fiance was a reincarnation of her former father. By karmic destiny, they were once again to share the same last name—this time as husband and wife.

Using the reasoning which was earlier applied to justify homosexuality, we can now see the same conclusion regarding incest. As we reverse the fact situation, if a father has sex with his daughter, maybe it's just a karmic holdover from a prior marriage of the same two entities.

We're told that, despite the veil of forgetfulness, we are

nevertheless the same entities which we were in former lives. So, if father and daughter had been previously married, they had already shared in a sexual relationship. Therefore, what we might consider to be incestuous is really all quite cosmic.

Am I unfairly taking reincarnationist logic too far? From *Dancing in the Light* it appears that Ms. MacLaine doesn't think so. When she and her Russian lover, Vassy, were fighting over her intimation that she was making love to him as if he were her son, she was confused:

> I had simply wanted to fantasize about being his mother while making love and to him this was some kind of fundamental evil?. . . Had I triggered some unconscious incestual fantasy that had actually attracted me to him in the first place?. . .
> Then, as I was sorting out my tumbled confusion, I had another flash. If we really had a past life experience together, could it have been as mother and son?

Can this bizarre path lead to a justification of child molestation, or even rape? Not only does reincarnationist logic agree, but Ms. MacLaine's supposed past lives also suggest such aberrational possibilities. After describing how she shared the bed of a bandit (who today is her mother), Ms. MacLaine tells what happened when a young man (her ex-husband in this life) raped her when she was pregnant:

> Yet I found I was enjoying the erotic struggle myself, my only concern being the welfare of the baby.

KARMIC THINKING IN SOCIETY

Shirley MacLaine does not personally advocate or approve of child molestation, incest, or rape. But philosophically based ideas invariably work their way into society, even if viewed initially as radically repugnant. The revolutionary acceptance of homosexuality and abortion are two good examples of how quickly societal attitudes and standards can change.

On the subject of abortion, Helen Wambach uses reincarnationist logic to conclude that there can be nothing morally wrong about abortion, because the only thing that is being killed is a *body*, not a soul:

> What light does this study shed on the question of abortion? . . . The soul apparently has a choice of which fetus to enter. If one fetus is aborted, apparently it is possible to choose another. In some cases, the soul who will occupy the fetus is in contact with the soul of the mother and can influence her decision regarding abortion.

If Wambach is to be believed, even the mother's decision may not be entirely her responsibility. Even more horrifying is the realization that, by implication, it shouldn't be wrong to murder *anyone*—fetus, infant, or adult—because it's just "killing a body, not a soul."

Wambach's follow-up comments raise some equally interesting implications:

> My data also indicates that souls can elect to leave

the fetus or the infant's body and return to the between-life state. Perhaps the sudden death syndrome in infants may be the result of a soul's decision not to go ahead with a life plan.

Without commenting on the crib-death hypothesis, I note with great curiosity what implication this possibility of one's choosing his or her existence might have regarding suicide. In other contexts we are told that suicide generates bad karma, yet suicide appears to be no different from the situation where, soon after birth, the soul decides to return to the between-life state. Using Wambach's reasoning, suicide is simply deciding not to go ahead with a life plan. (When I asked Kevin Ryerson if that is an accurate reincarnationist position regarding suicide, without hesitation or qualification he agreed.)

And perhaps, through euthanasia, we can do another soul a favor by terminating one's miserable existence, letting him get on to a better situation in another lifetime. Even a killing with *bad* intent will eventually, on the cosmic scale of things, work itself out for both the murderer and his victim. And why wouldn't that work globally as well, if we decided it was in our best interest to drop the bomb?

John-Roger, a Los Angeles "spiritual leader" in the "Movement of Spiritual Inner Awareness," carries this further:

Let's look at the Vietnamese people for the last 3,000 years of their existence. As a collective group, they may have gotten exactly what they created for themselves, and they may have balanced all of their karma. Now, is it bad for them to be karmically free of all that? Is that wrong? Perhaps that particular freedom didn't come about in a really popular way, in terms of what we all might have wanted it to be, but it came about in a way that was entirely perfect. There was no overkill; there was no underkill.

The Americans that went over there and were caught up in it were part of the Vietnamese process thousands of years ago, and even though they were born in America this life, they were pulled back there to complete their karma, also. And those who went through the war unharmed were not part of the process and came home safely. So how can that action be judged as "wrong"?

At last—a reasonable explanation for the war in Vietnam! The young men who were killed in Vietnam were meeting their own karma, and it was also karmic napalm which was dropped on the enemy. Perhaps, then, our involvement in Central America is also cosmically ordained!

DEVALUING HUMAN LIFE

It looks as if there is no end to karmic rationalization. It may even reach genocidal proportions, if W. H. Church and Edgar Cayce are right. In his book, *Many Happy Returns: The Lives of Edgar Cayce*, Church says:

> Evidently the ancient forefathers of the American Indians were those sons of Belial of old, who escaped from a doomed Atlantis to what is now the American continent. And the arriving settlers, if we interpret Cayce's words aright, were none

other than the former children of the Law of One, "coming again into the closer relationships and contact." If true, it tells us much about the tragic and bloody conflicts between European settlers and Indians that later arose out of that karmic reunion of opposing forces.

If it's all karmic, then why should we even characterize the annihilation of the American Indians as "tragic?" It sounds like those "sons of Belial" got what they deserved! Is it just coincidence, or is there in all this reincarnationist talk a significant *devaluation of human life*—from abortion, to crib deaths, to suicide, to war, to genocide? Is it also just coincidence that, as the market drops on human value, animal value is on the rise? Ms. MacLaine's higher self told her:

> We humans should never forget our capacity to connect with the collective spirit of animals. Their energy is essential to our future growth. The animals are on the earth for a reason and our disrespect for them has become alarming.

And is it just coincidence that the clamor for animal rights comes at a time when human life has been so karmically cheapened? You can kill a human fetus almost at your own whim because it supposedly does not yet contain a soul, but you can't kill animals even for medical research because, as Ms. MacLaine puts it, "pulsating in their collective consciousness are the lessons of the past."

If Ms. MacLaine and other New Age proponents are really looking for enlightenment, and if today's reincarnationists are serious about their spiritual evolution, they must ask some hard questions about the direction in which they are headed. The social and ethical standards which are coming from their philosophy surely must be an embarrassment. Yet, given the accepted premises, the conclusions logically follow.

The moral and sociological spin-offs from the idea of reincarnation convince me that the law of karma has at least this grain of truth: There is indeed cause and effect between the basic life premise which one chooses to believe and the kinds of personal and societal standards that result. As they keep telling us, if we want to know why there is a given effect, we must look at the cause. With this much I agree: Low standards don't come from high teachings.

CHAPTER FOURTEEN
ONCE FOR ETERNITY

"Death is the opening of a more subtle life. In the flower, it sets free the perfume; in the chrysalis, the butterfly; in man, the soul."

—JULIETTE ADAM

IF I CAN EXPECT TO LIVE ONLY ONCE on this earth, what can I expect to happen when I die? What kind of an afterlife can I anticipate? Is heaven really anything more than pie in the sky? Is it more than just a setting for endless Saint Peter jokes? In heaven, will we really be like angels? And what about hell? Is there really a horrible place of punishment for the wicked? Don't the wicked merely experience a living hell on earth?

So many questions crowd in for attention when one thinks ahead to death and to what will happen in the unseen world beyond. Even though the process of dying carries some dread —particularly in instances associated with pain and suffering—death itself should cause no fear. Ms. MacLaine and I agree about that. In death we merely discard the human body. The soul lives on. We will continue to exist. I believe this, not because I fear any finality in death and therefore seek immortality, but because, through Christ, I have the hope of even greater personal fulfillment in the life to come.

Heaven has been so casually treated that few people take

it seriously anymore. Perhaps this is because we live in such an affluent society that we think we already have a heaven on earth. Or perhaps it is because we have difficulty conceptualizing anything beyond our present existence. Biblical references to "streets of gold" and "pearly gates," whatever they may actually turn out to be, are telling us that heaven will be glorious, beyond our imagination. God used language we can understand from our present existence in order to get across concepts that our minds cannot fully grasp. What we know about heaven is that it is something to look forward to, that it is so wonderful no one would want to miss it.

Through the descriptions given to us of heaven, we are promised that we will not have to endure any of the pain or suffering or death that we are familiar with in this life. There will be no bad karma to work off, no sin to overcome. We won't have to worry about being reassigned to this world as a deformed child, a Hindu untouchable, or a victim of discrimination.

"But what will we *do*?" someone asks. "Won't we be bored silly living in heaven for an eternity?" Perhaps it is particularly difficult for those of us who live in an activity-oriented, schedule-filled, and clock-watching society to appreciate how different eternity will be. Eternity is not so much a matter of time or quantity, but of quality. It's the difference between saying, "She lived only 28 years," and saying, "She was a gifted, fulfilled, and happy woman." It's the difference between saying, "I've been in 25 countries," and saying, "I have learned tremendous lessons from the people I have met in my travels." Eternal life is a quality which Christians take on even in this present existence. Jesus said, "I tell you the truth, whoever hears my word and believes him who sent me [already] *has* eternal life. . . he *has* [already] crossed over from death to life."

Seen in that light, what we will *do* in heaven seems secondary and insignificant. While two people who love each other might enjoy planning an exciting venture, it hardly matters what they actually *do* while they are together. Just *being together* is what they are really looking forward to. As Ms. MacLaine pointed out so well regarding those who are "doers" and those who are "be-ers," it is *being* that is most fulfilling, not *doing*. Christians look forward eagerly to the rich sharing of fellowship with God and with each other.

Part of our difficulty in understanding heaven is that we are not yet ready for it. God must talk to us as children because we still have an immature view of what life and afterlife is all about. There was a time for each of us when the creativity and pleasure of planting delicate little flowers in a backyard garden would have been lost on us as children, content simply to play in the dirt. Heaven, for those of us who are adults, will be as qualitatively superior to this life as adulthood is to childhood. And is there any way for an adult to *explain* that to a child?

In whatever way they might define it, most people want to go to heaven when they die. By contrast, I can't say that I know *anyone* who wants to end up in hell. In fact, most people want to dismiss that possibility altogether. But Jesus warns us that hell exists, and that hell is not just another word, like hades, for the unseen world. Whatever else hell is, it is clearly a place of punishment which must never be explained away or ignored.

The description of hell puts anyone on notice that it is a terrible destiny. By comparison with a heavenly life of immeasurable personal fulfillment, hell will be a severe penalty indeed. In his divine revelation, John tells us that, "The lake of fire is the second death. If anyone's name was not found written in the book of life, he was thrown into the lake of fire."

As with heaven, any attempt to fully comprehend hell must be inadequate. But I think I get a slight inkling of what hell might be like when I fail to follow directions in storing my work on the computer word processor and end up erasing five hours of writing. There is a helpless, frustrating, sickening feeling you have when the screen flashes the words: "Not found." "Not found."

Unfortunately, some of my former students have experienced a similar feeling when they searched in vain for their name to appear in the list of those who had passed the Bar Exam. When at last they have turned away in utter disappointment, all they could think of was the fact that their name was not found. "Not found." What a bitter contrast the rejection of hell will be, compared with the promise made to the person who has submitted his life to the lordship of Christ. For Christ has promised, "I will never erase his name from the book of life, but will acknowledge his name before my Father and his angels."

David told Ms. MacLaine that "Even religion believes in cause and effect—that's why, when they threw out reincarnation, they dreamt up heaven and hell to take care of all the unfulfilled effects." At least David and I agree that some way, somehow, there will be a judgment of our attitudes and actions in this life. But it will not be on the *impersonal* basis of cause and effect. If it were, there would be no need for heaven, because no one would qualify. Nobody's perfect. Fortunately for those who have chosen Christ as their Savior, when it comes to adding up our sins, God has promised his children that he will forget all the wrong they ever did!

But if there *is* a hell for those who vehemently deny the lordship of Jesus Christ, who arrogantly assume the attributes of deity as did Satan before them, and who cynically dismiss the very idea of hell as a possibility, then one can only hope, for their sakes, that they are wrong about cause and effect. The last thing any of them would want to encounter in hell is cause and effect meticulously applied.

✦

A NEW ETERNAL BODY

Despite all that I have said so far, I must confess that I do believe in reincarnation.

Once.

It will happen at the time of the resurrection. At the resurrection, when Jesus Christ comes again to the earth to reclaim his own, the faithful who have already died will be raised from the dead. Then, says Paul, the faithful who are alive at the time of the resurrection will be caught up with them to meet the Lord, with whom they all will enter into heaven (1 Thessalonians 4:13-18).

That is when our *one-time* reincarnation will take place. The soul that has been incarnated in the earthly body, and which has been separated from the corruptible body at death, will enter into a new, eternal body. Paul explained to the Corinthian Christians that the new body is not going to be like the body with which we are presently familiar (1 Corinthians 15:35-57). Paul says that we must be careful how we view it. He reminds us that when we plant a seed, the new life which comes from it is in a form quite different from the seed itself.

He also reminds us that there are many different kinds of bodies, each designed perfectly for its unique purpose. In this world, humans have one kind of body, animals have other kinds of bodies, birds other kinds, and fish still others. Even the "heavenly bodies" in our present universe—the moon, the stars, and the planets—all have different sizes, shapes, and brilliance.

The most important thing to consider, says Paul, is that there can be both corruptible physical bodies, such as we now have, and incorruptible spiritual bodies, as we one day will have. As descendants of Adam, everyone has received a mortal physical body. In the next life the spiritual heirs of Christ will each receive an immortal spiritual body. Just as our present bodies were created perfect for the environment in which we exist here on the earth, so our eternal bodies will be exactly what we need for our eternal existence. In our new form, we will be as much like the eternal Christ as we have been like the mortal Adam.

Our new bodies will be as different from our present bodies as a butterfly is different from the wormlike caterpillar. We know that every butterfly goes through four stages in its life: egg, larva (caterpillar), pupa, and adult. During each stage its appearance changes and it leads a completely different kind of life. The process of growth and development through its several forms is called metamorphosis.

Like the egg of the developing butterfly, we spend the first months of existence as an embryo in our mother's womb. Then, like the caterpillar, we grow from childhood to adulthood in an existence of awareness, learning, and nonstop activity. When we die we pass through the cocoon of death and become the most beautiful creatures we could ever imagine.

We have much to gain from being in the eternal state. No longer will we be the destructive larva of humankind that we now are. Whatever body we have in heaven will prevent that from happening. And, as for the question of what we will do—just think of the freedom!

But can't you just hear some of the caterpillars

philosophizing between munches on a leaf? "Why in the world would any caterpillar *want* to live beyond the cocoon?" "And what would we *do* if we did?" "I'd just as soon come back again like I am, and have another go at this leaf."

✦

NEW LIFE NOW!

Spiritual metamorphosis is what it's all about. Not reincarnation. Not evolution. Not self-awareness within a deteriorating earthly body. As the crowning glory of God's creation, we have a distinct advantage over caterpillars and butterflies: Our metamorphosis can begin even in *this* life! We can become new persons while living in the same body! That's what spiritual rebirth is all about. As Christians, we become new creatures in Christ—now, in this life, before we die, on this side of heaven.

If our bodies are like packages, as Ms. MacLaine agrees, then we don't need *more* packages. What we need is to change the person we presently are inside our package. Again Shirley agrees, but insists that we need *many* bodies (*more time*) to change what's inside.

If a person is physically handicapped, we wait for him, if necessary, to do what others could do more quickly. But giving him more time won't eliminate the handicap that he faces. If it were somehow possible to eliminate his handicap altogether, then he would never again need more time. Eliminating our handicaps is what God's grace does when we commit ourselves to him in obedient faith.

We don't have to wait for heaven in order to become a new spiritual person. In fact, if we do, it will be too late. By committing our lives to Christ and following his teaching, we are transformed (metamorphosized), even now, by the renewing of our minds and the rebirth of our spirits.

The reincarnationists often misuse Jesus' reference to "many mansions" to picture the cycle of human bodies that a soul must go through on its way to spiritual enlightenment. The more accurate picture, from a biblical perspective, is of *one* mansion with more than one spirit. For the Christian, there is more than one spirit within his "package." He is not alone in his body: His body is also a dwelling for God's Spirit, which fills, fulfills, transforms, and loves.

Eventually one gets the message: Better to live in one dilapidated house filled with companionship and love than in a succession of comfortable "mansions" alone. In this truth Christianity is far superior to Eastern mysticism. While mystics, through their mantras and meditation, are alone and talking to themselves, the Christian, through prayer, is talking to a constant companion—the Creator God of the universe.

COMPARE THE CONSEQUENCES

When all the mind games are played, and all the courtroom logic is expended, what really counts is how our beliefs affect our lives and the lives of those around us. Shirley MacLaine and I can easily jet off to Peru, or India, or China—wherever we want—and use the time to gain spiritual perspective for ourselves. And we can just as easily return to our comfortable lifestyles in Malibu and indulge in wild, speculative theories. But the millions of people we leave behind in squalor, ignorance, hunger, and the day-to-day uncertainties of life don't have the luxury of doing that.

The people of the world need a personal God to sustain them, and maybe the rich and famous *even more so.* Turning to the impersonal law of karma and its insensitive enforcer—reincarnation—leaves neither the rich nor the poor with a God who can love, comfort, forgive, or fulfill. The God who can do all this is personal and real. He greatly desires fellowship with us, and thereby greatly honors us.

Having made us in his own image, God is saddened and disappointed when we rebel against him through lives filled with sin. Even so, God has not abandoned us or angrily retaliated against us. Instead, "God so loved the world that he gave his one and only Son, that whoever believes in him shall not perish but have eternal life. For God did not send his Son into the world to condemn the world, but to save the world through him" (John 3:16,17).

Our salvation came at an awful price, the death of Jesus on the cross. His death came that we might have life. His blood was shed so that our sins could be forgiven. Men and women have died cruel deaths for good causes, but Jesus was the sinless Son of God, and he died for the greatest cause of all—our eternal salvation. It is because of his love and ultimate sacrifice that we give allegiance to Christ Jesus:

> Who, being in very nature God, did not consider equality with God something to be grasped, but made himself nothing, taking the very nature of a servant, being made in human likeness. And being found in appearance as a man, he humbled himself and became obedient to death—even death on a cross! Therefore God exalted him to the highest place and gave him the name that is above every name, that at the name of Jesus every knee should bow, in heaven and on earth and under the earth, and every tongue confess that Jesus Christ is Lord, to the glory of God the Father (Philippians 2:6-11).

In Christ we can live our lives confidently, knowing that God will never abandon us.

> Who shall separate us from the love of Christ? Shall trouble or hardship or persecution or famine or nakedness or danger or sword?... No, in all these things we are more than conquerors through him who loved us. For I am convinced that neither death nor life, neither angels nor demons, neither the present nor the future, nor any powers, neither height nor depth, nor anything else in all creation, will be able to separate us from the love of God that is in Christ Jesus our Lord (Romans 8:35-39).

FINDING THE TRUE LIGHT

With such hope and assurance through Christ, why should we look to any other source for security and fulfillment? Why should we trust our own efforts to "get it right"? Ms. MacLaine's eclectic philosophy of reincarnation and selfism, and her belief in trance mediums, UFO's, and extraterrestrials, is fascination fraught with danger. Adopting such a speculative belief system is like skydiving without a parachute.

Paul gives this caution to those who are already Christians, and these words of eternal importance to those who have not yet committed their lives to Christ:

> See to it that no one takes you captive through hollow and deceptive philosophy, which depends on human tradition and the basic principles of this world rather than on Christ.
>
> For in Christ all the fullness of the Deity lives in bodily form, and you have been given fullness in

Christ, who is the head over every power and authority. . . .

When you were dead in your sins. . .God made you alive with Christ. . . .

Since, then, you have been raised with Christ, set your hearts on things above, where Christ is seated at the right hand of God. Set your minds on things above, not on earthly things. For you died, and your life is now hidden with Christ in God. When Christ, who is your life, appears, then you also will appear with him in glory (Colossians 2:8ff.).

Can believing in the impersonal law of karma possibly bring meaning to your existence in this life? Does the notion of reincarnation bring out the best in you? Can you find fulfillment in the mind-expansion trips of the New Age movement? Are you happiest when you are wrapped up in yourself?

It would be one thing to go out on a limb to believe in reincarnation and selfism if that belief had no serious consequences. But where the stakes are so high, as in the meaning of life and afterlife, and where the alternative of life in Christ is so clearly and freely given, what sense does it make to risk your destiny both now and forever? Why would anyone want to go dancing in the dark out on a broken limb?

I am the light of the world.
Whoever follows me will never walk in darkness,
but will have the light of life.

—Jesus Christ